THE AWESOME ACTIVITY ADVENTURE BOOK

FEATURING KOW KAPOW AND THE BONSAI KID!

BEACH

BARRON'S

BEACH WOULD LIKE TO THANK
LISA, RICHARD, CAT, AND NIKALAS

FIRST EDITION FOR THE UNITED STATES, ITS TERRITORIES AND DEPENDENCIES,
AND CANADA PUBLISHED IN 2012 BY BARRON'S EDUCATIONAL SERIES, INC.

TEXT AND ILLUSTRATIONS ©COPYRIGHT BEACH 2010

THE RIGHT OF BEACH TO BE IDENTIFIED AS THE AUTHOR AND ILLUSTRATOR OF THIS WORK HAS
BEEN ASSERTED BY HIM IN ACCORDANCE WITH THE COPYRIGHT, PATENTS, AND DESIGN ACT, 1988.

PUBLISHED IN THE UNITED KINGDOM BY SCHOLASTIC LTD.
SCHOLASTIC CHILDREN'S BOOKS
EUSTON HOUSE
24 EVERSHOLT STREET
LONDON, NW1 1DB
UNITED KINGDOM

EDITORIAL DIRECTOR: LISA EDWARDS
EDITOR: CATRIONA CLARKE

ALL INQUIRIES SHOULD BE ADDRESSED TO:
BARRON'S EDUCATIONAL SERIES, INC.
250 WIRELESS BOULEVARD
HAUPPAUGE, NY 11788
WWW.BARRONSEDUC.COM

LIBRARY OF CONGRESS CONTROL NUMBER: 2011930877

ISBN-13: 978-1-4380-0084-8

DATE OF MANUFACTURE: JUNE 2012
MANUFACTURED BY: LO8EO80, KOWLOON, HONG KONG, CHINA

9 8 7 6 5 4 3 2

CONTENTS

DOWN ON THE FUNNY FARM 5
ROBOT FACTORY 35
ZANY ZOO 65
PERILOUS PIRATES 95
DEEP SEA DISCO 125
CREEPY CASTLE 155
SUPERHERO CITY 185
CRAZY CARS 215
THE MOOVELLOUS MILKY WAY 243
THE INTERGALACTIC GAMES 271
PUZZLE AND QUIZ ANSWERS 300

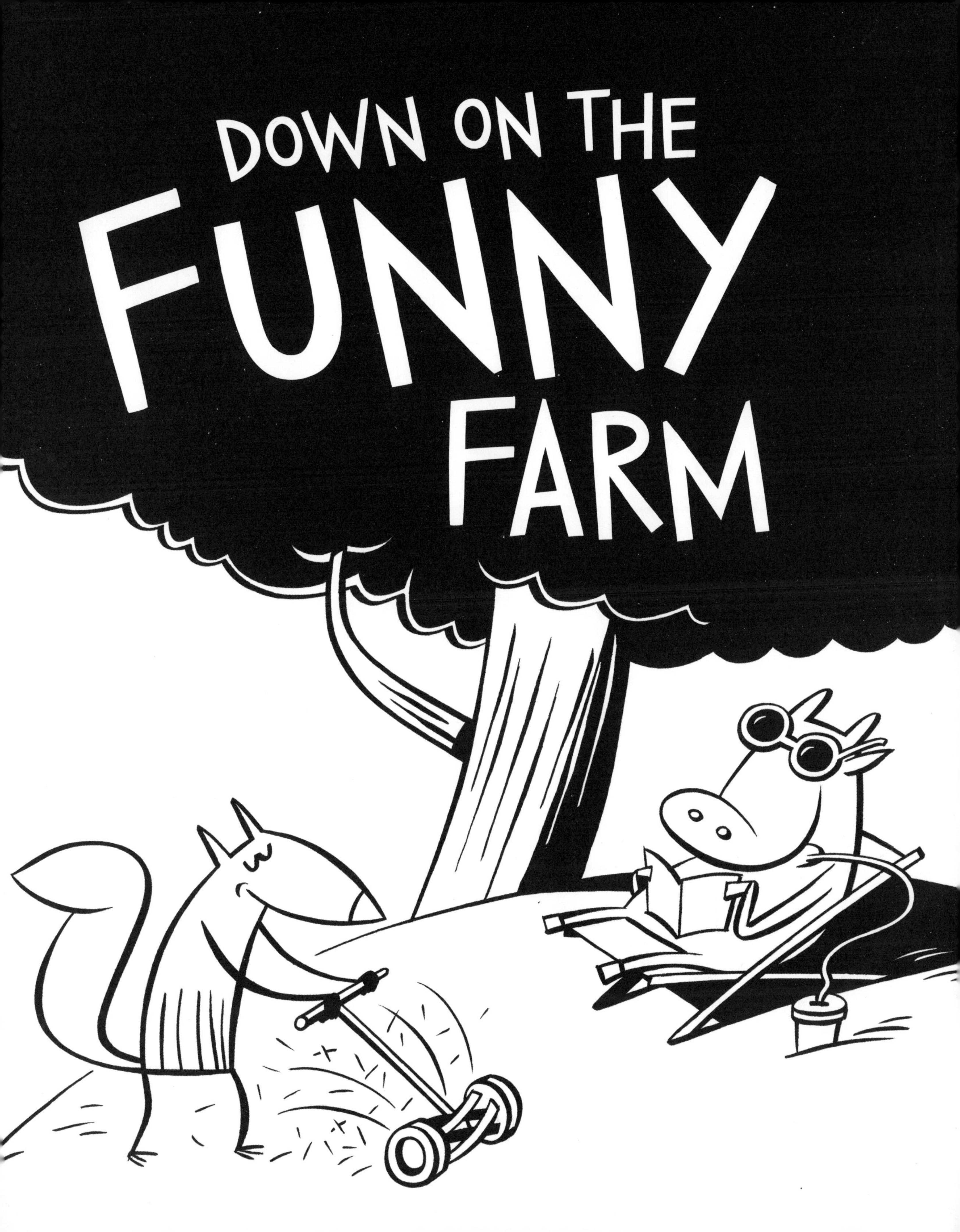
DOWN ON THE
FUNNY
FARM

AND THE BONSAI KID

AND NOT FORGETTING..

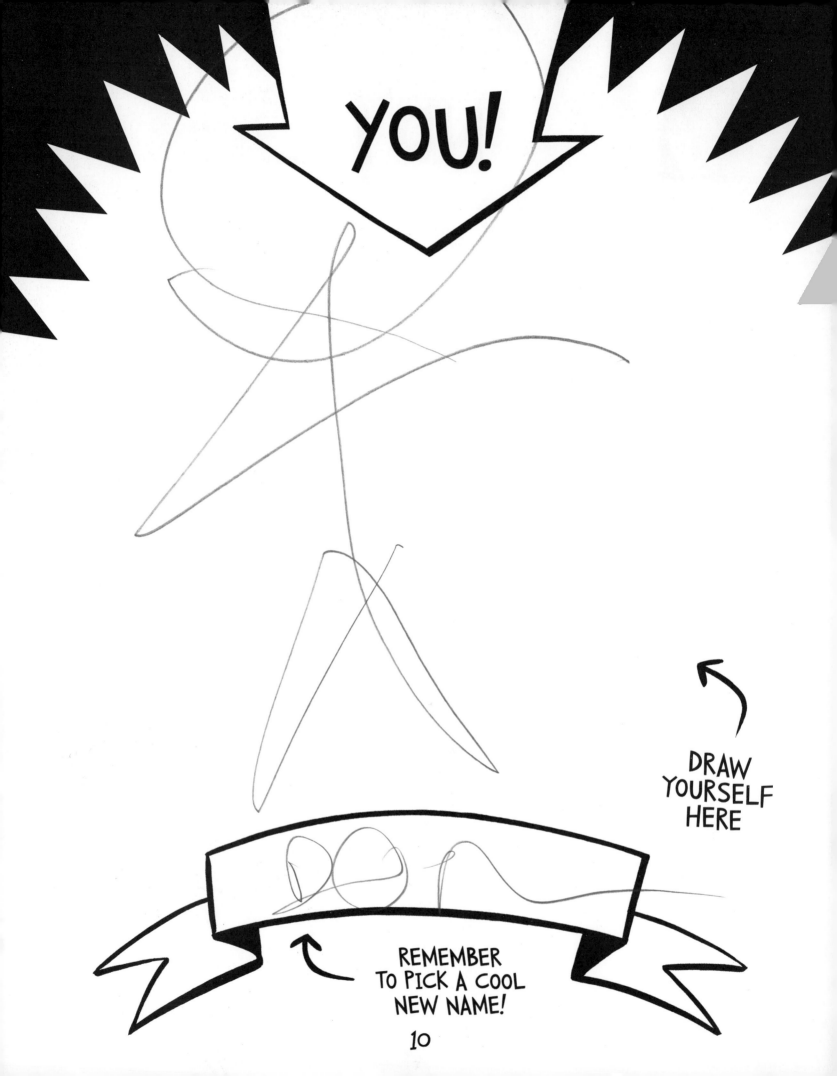

CONNECT THE FLIES TO REVEAL A SMELLY CARTOON!

SCRATCH
AND SNIFF
FARMYARD
SMELLS
PAGE

BEST BEFORE 1988

DRAW YOUR OWN
FART HERE!

15

DRAW A BIG SCARECROW
TO SHOO AWAY
THE BIRDS

NOW DRAW THE UGLIEST
FARMER YOU CAN
THINK OF

HE WAS SHORT AND FAT WITH AN ENORMOUS RED MOUSTACHE THAT CURLED UP AT EACH END. HE HAD THICK BROWN HAIR, A STUBBLY CHIN, AND EYEBROWS SO BUSHY YOU COULD BUILD A NEST IN THEM.

WANTED

DRAW THE THIEF THAT EACH WITLESS WITNESS DESCRIBES

HE WAS TALL AND THIN WITH EYES AS BIG AS ELEPHANT EGGS. HE HAD A POINTY BLUE BEARD, A CROOKED NOSE, AND LONG THIN HAIR. MY FRIEND SAID HE LOOKED JUST LIKE THAT MAN FROM THE TV, BUT I SAID I ONLY LISTEN TO THE RADIO.

WANTED

22

COLOR IN THE DOTTED AREAS TO REVEAL THE VILLAIN!

24

HARD

BECOME A BLACK BELT
IN SUDOKU!

JUST FILL IN THE SQUARES SO THAT EVERY LINE
ACROSS AND EVERY LINE DOWN CONTAINS THE
NUMBERS 1-9. IF YOU GET IT RIGHT, EACH BIG BOX
OF NINE SQUARES WILL ALSO CONTAIN ONLY THE
NUMBERS 1-9

26

```
S H E E P D O G A T G U
C B A R N J Y S T R A W
A H M Y T E P L O W G H
R P I G S T Y T J G W E
E E L C I T R H C P R E
C W K V K C A A O L N L
R E M F D E Q C C O M B
O O A I O B N R K T I A
W I I V N J C E E U O R
Q N D D K H F A R M E R
H O R S E S H O E M Z O
Y T S B Y F I E L D T W
```

EASY

CAN YOU FIND THE WORDS HIDDEN
ON THE SIDE OF THIS GETAWAY TRUCK?

TRACTOR	SCARECROW	PIGSTY	STRAW
HAYSTACK	HORSESHOE	COCKEREL	WHEELBARROW
SHEEPDOG	CHICKEN	BARN	PLOW
FARMER	MILKMAID	FIELD	DONKEY

DRAW THE ANIMALS
THAT MADE THESE
FOOTPRINTS

28

ANSWER EACH CLUE TO COMPLETE THIS CACTUS CROSSWORD!

ACROSS
4. THE BONSAI KID SAYS THE CHICKENS ARE FEATHER-BRAINED... (7)
5. A SMELLY PUDDLE OF POO (6)
7. A PAIR OF THESE LANDED ON KOW'S HEAD (5)

DOWN
1. KOW'S SPECIAL BIRTHDAY TREAT (6,3,8)
2. KOW AND THE KID WANT TO KICK SOME OF THIS! (5)
3. THE SOUND A HAYSTACK HIDER SOMETIMES MAKES (3)
6. THE KID LANDED IN A BOX OF THESE (4)

DRAW THE
INHABITANTS
OF THIS
FIELD

DANGER!
MAN-
EATING
PLANTS!

SPOT THE DIFFERENCE!

CAN YOU FIND THE 10 DIFFERENCES BETWEEN THESE TWO PICTURES?

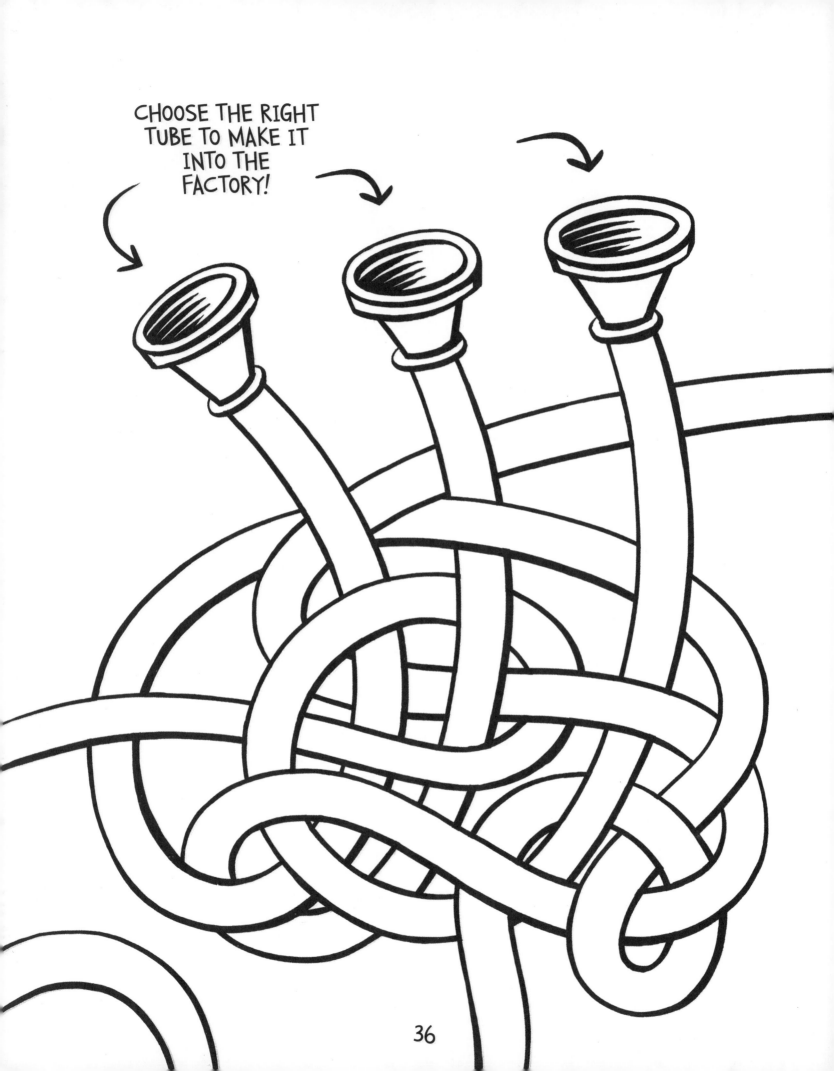

DRAW THE
BIGGEST, BADDEST
ROBOT YOU CAN
THINK OF

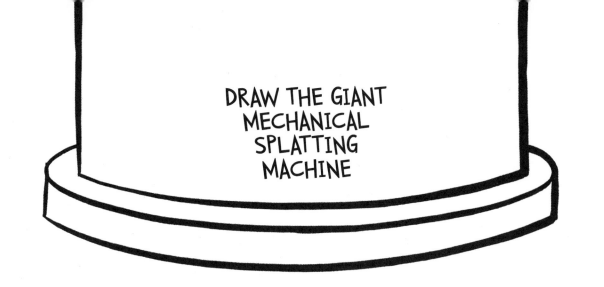

DRAW THE GIANT
MECHANICAL
SPLATTING
MACHINE

THIS ROBOT HAS MALFUNCTIONED—CAN YOU UNJUMBLE HIM?

S C R E W D R I V E R W
J O T L J E W D P L C S
U S F A C T O R Y E O P
L C I T Z H N B M C M A
R A I A W B G I J T P N
E N S R H A M M E R U N
P N I E C A R O B O T E
A E G K R U N E P N E R
I R M A U Y I D O I R A
R S Z R D N R T R C Q L
E K V X B G F T X O K Z
A W I B Q Z E O C H I P
H K S P B A T T E R Y D

ANDROID   GADGET   REPAIR   SPANNER
ELECTRONIC   ROBOT   HAMMER   SCREWDRIVER
COMPUTER   CIRCUIT   **EASY**   CHIP   FACTORY
LASER   SCANNER   SOFTWARE   BATTERY

DESIGN A RUSTY ROBOT-REPAIRING MACHINE!

DRAW THE
ROBOT THAT THE
BONSAI KID
IS FIGHTING

NOW ADD
THE ROBOT THAT
KOW KAPOW
IS FIGHTING

WHAT IS THIS SECURITY
GUARD WATCHING?

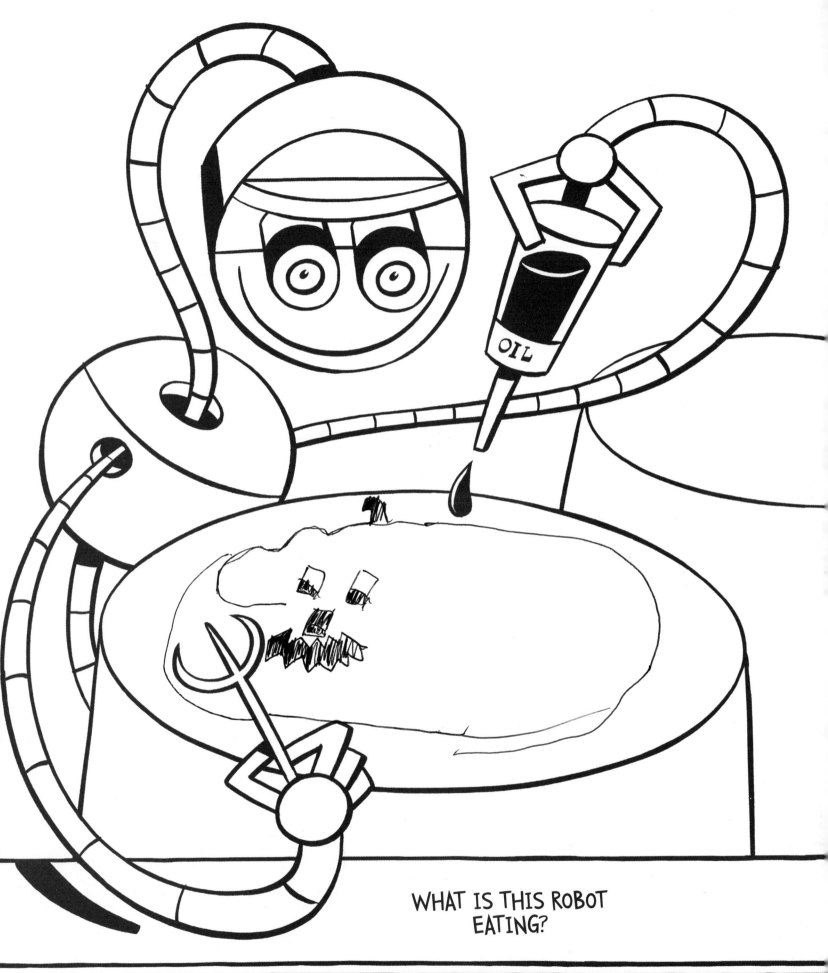

WHAT IS THIS ROBOT
EATING?

FILL IN THE SQUARES SO THAT EVERY ROW,
EVERY COLUMN, AND EVERY 2 x 2 BOX
CONTAINS THE NUMBERS 1, 2, 3, AND 4

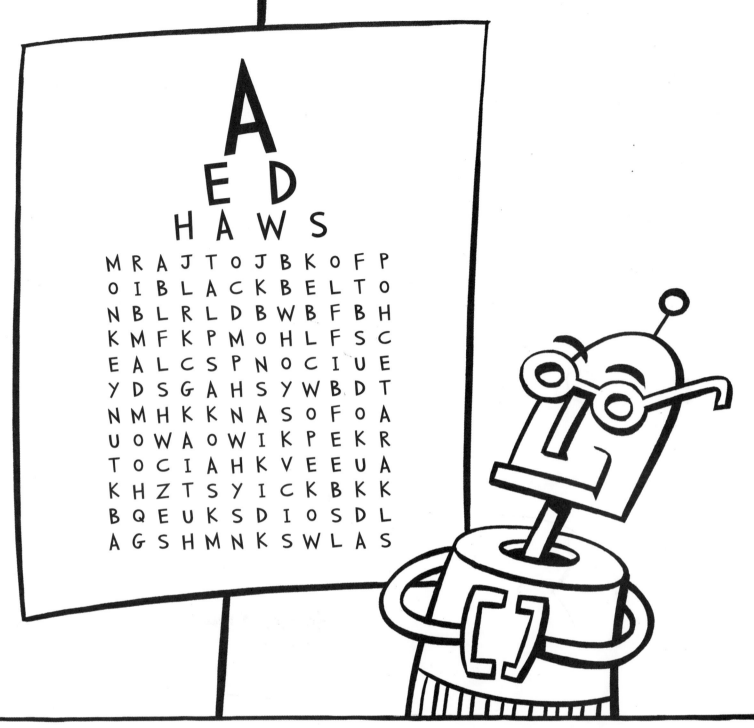

A
E D
H A W S

```
M R A J T O J B K O F P
O I B L A C K B E L T O
N B L R L D B W B F B H
K M F K P M O H L F S C
E A L C S P N O C I U E
Y D S G A H S Y W B D T
N M H K K N A S O F O A
U O W A O W I K P E K R
T O C I A H K V E E U A
K H Z T S Y I C K B K K
B Q E U K S D I O S D L
A G S H M N K S W L A S
```

KOW KAPOW   KARATE CHOP   FAIR   MILKSHAKE   MAD MOO
BONSAI KID   MONKEY NUT   BEEF BIFF   KA-SPLAT
SUSHI SWISH   BLACK BELT   GETAWAY   SUDOKU

INTERMISSION

FIGHTING ROBOTS AND CHASING MONKEY NUTS
CAN BE THIRSTY WORK—TIME FOR A SHORT
BREAK FROM THE ACTION AND A WORD
FROM OUR SPONSORS...

TOP SECRET

FACT FILE:

KOW KAPOW

aka
The Milkshake
Moover

PROFILE:

Body of a cow, mind of a ninja, fart of a foghorn.

Trained under Mr. Mooyagi at the Deadly Donut Dojo from the age of 3.

Blackbelt in Karate, Judo, and Eating With Chopsticks.

Signature fighting move : Ten Ton Wonton
Star sign : Taurus
Favorite film : High School Moosical
Weakness : Slightly ticklish behind left ear...

HOW TO DRAW KOW KAPOW

FOLLOW THE STEP-BY-STEP GUIDE TO CREATE THE PERFECT COW CARTOON! THE BLACK LINES SHOW YOU WHAT TO DRAW FOR EACH STEP AND THE GREY LINES SHOW WHAT YOU'VE ALREADY DONE.

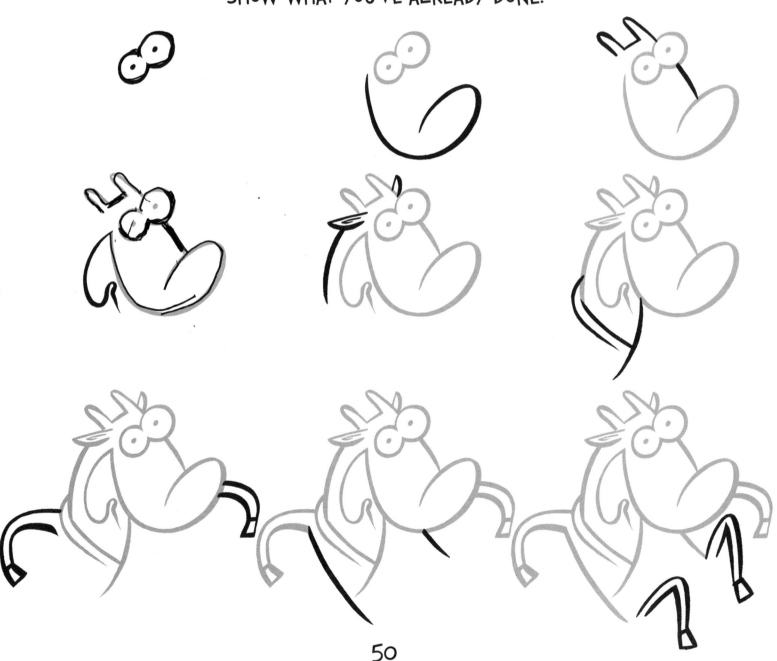

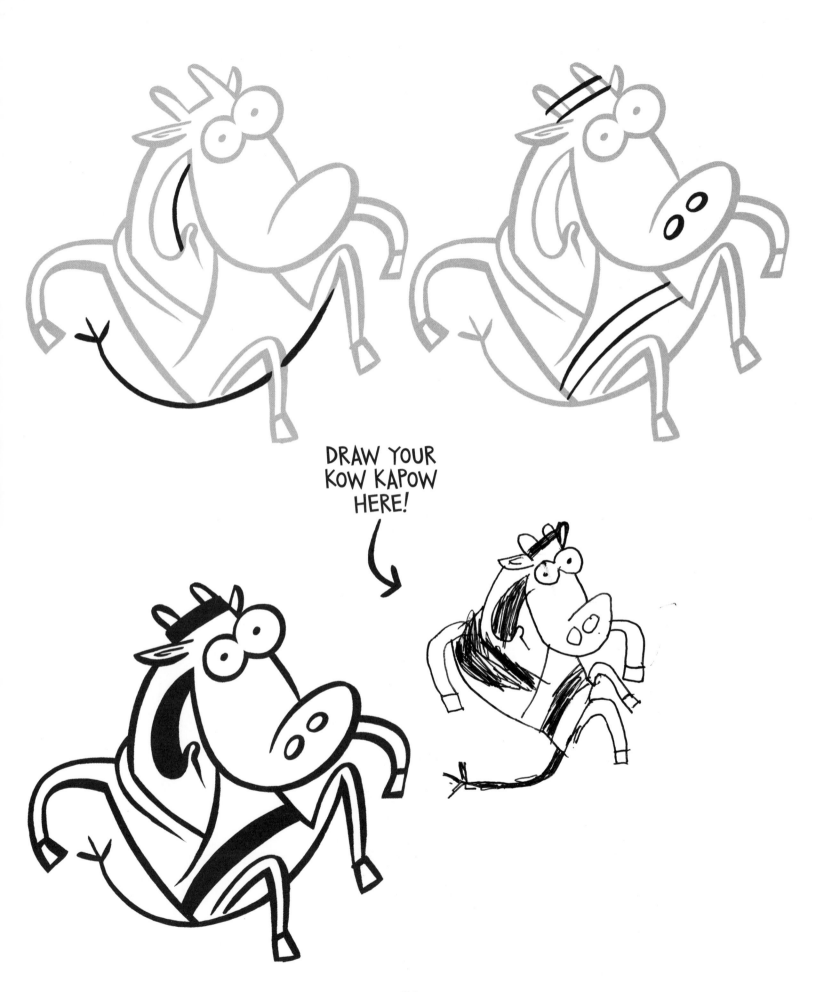

DRAW YOUR
KOW KAPOW
HERE!

HOW TO MAKE YOUR OWN CARTOON STRIP

FIRST WE NEED SOME ACTORS!

MATCH THE WORDS BELOW IN ANY ORDER TO CREATE A NEW CAST OF CHARACTERS FOR YOUR CARTOON.

FLYING	WIDGET	RABBIT
KUNG FU	NINJA	WIZARD
WACKY	LASER	KITTEN
BURPING	PANCAKE	BOY
SUPERSTAR	GLITTER	MONKEY
CHOCOLATE	FRIDGE	MAN
SHINY	KARAOKE	BUG
PING PONG	FART	GIRL
SPINNING	HIP HOP	PIG
X-RAY	FLIP FLOP	FROG
GINGER	ROLLER	DUCK
CRUNCHY	HAIRCUT	KING

52

NOW DRAW THEM ON THESE PODIUMS!

BATMAN

NOW FOR THE STORY
—THIS IS THE EASY BIT!

WHERE

THINK OF A LOCATION FOR YOUR COMIC

- IN THE SCHOOL PLAYGROUND
- AT THE TOP OF A MOUNTAIN
- IN THE CUPBOARD UNDER THE KITCHEN SINK

WHO

NOW DREAM UP SOME CHARACTERS

- AN EVIL AUNTY
- A TALKING PET
- A BRAIN-EATING ZOMBIE
- A ZOMBIE-EATING BRAIN

WHAT

WHAT ARE THEY DOING?

- PLAYING FOOTBALL
- FLIPPING PANCAKES
- HOLDING A SMELLIEST FART COMPETITION
- BUILDING A ROBOT TEACHER

WHY

AND WHY ARE THEY DOING IT?

- TO EARN SOME EXTRA POCKET MONEY
- TO IMPROVE THE SCHOOL
- TO TAKE OVER THE WORLD

WRITE DOWN ALL
YOUR IDEAS
HERE

NOW HERE ARE SOME PANELS TO DRAW YOUR OWN CARTOON!

TITLE
GOES
HERE

THE END!

SHOW YOUR COMIC
TO SOMEONE ELSE...

WHAT DO YOUR
READERS
THINK?

AND NOW
BACK TO THE
ACTION!

64

OH NO!

CAN YOU HELP KOW AND THE BONSAI KID
FIND THEIR WAY TO THE TICKET OFFICE?

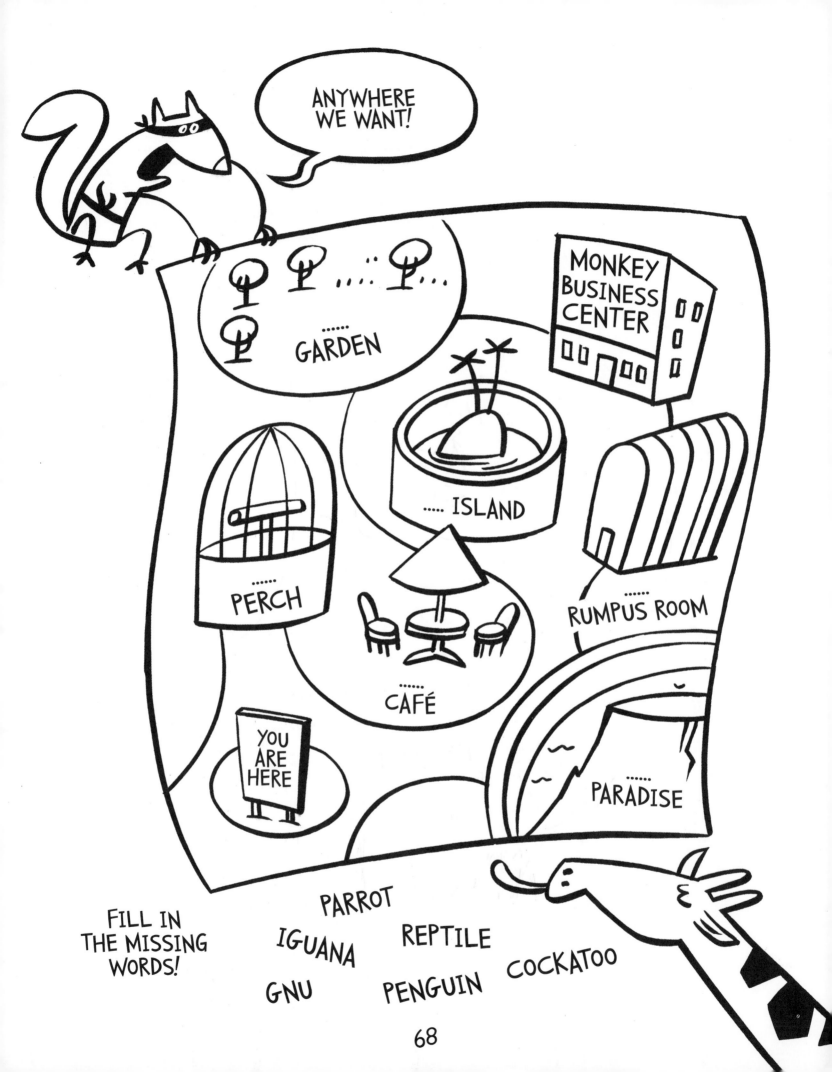

WHICH ANIMAL LIVES IN
THIS ENCLOSURE?

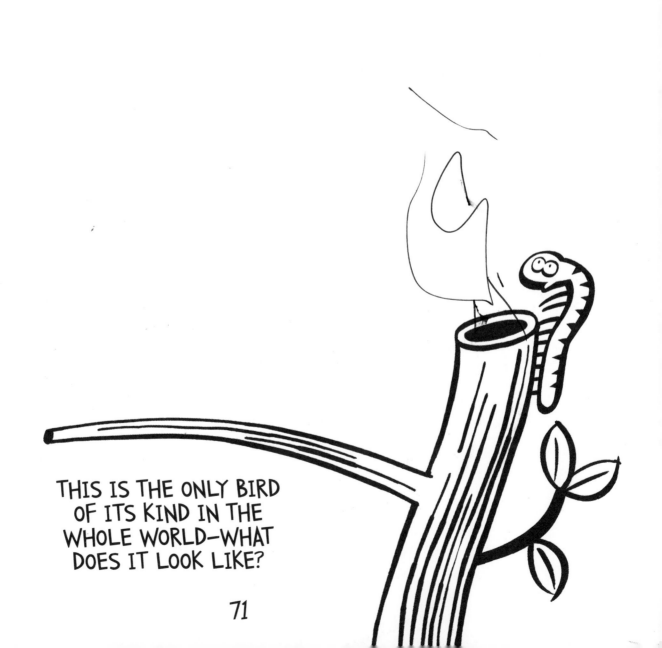

THIS IS THE ONLY BIRD
OF ITS KIND IN THE
WHOLE WORLD—WHAT
DOES IT LOOK LIKE?

CONNECT THE FLEAS ON THIS LION'S BACK TO
REVEAL ANOTHER CREATURE.

WHAT IS THIS CROC CRUNCHING?

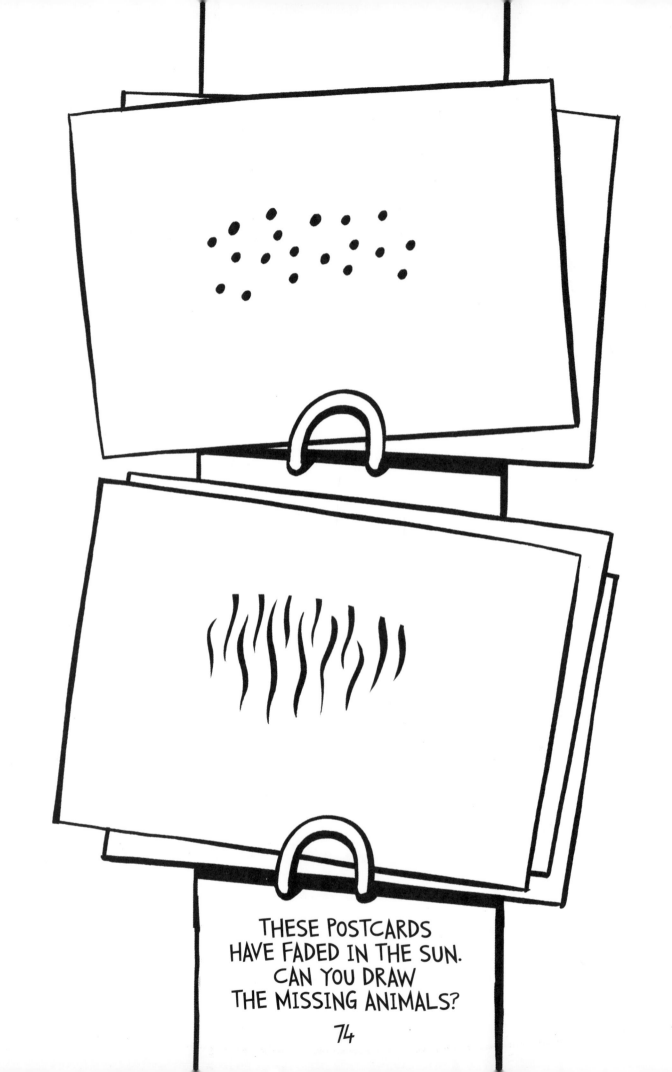

THESE POSTCARDS
HAVE FADED IN THE SUN.
CAN YOU DRAW
THE MISSING ANIMALS?

74

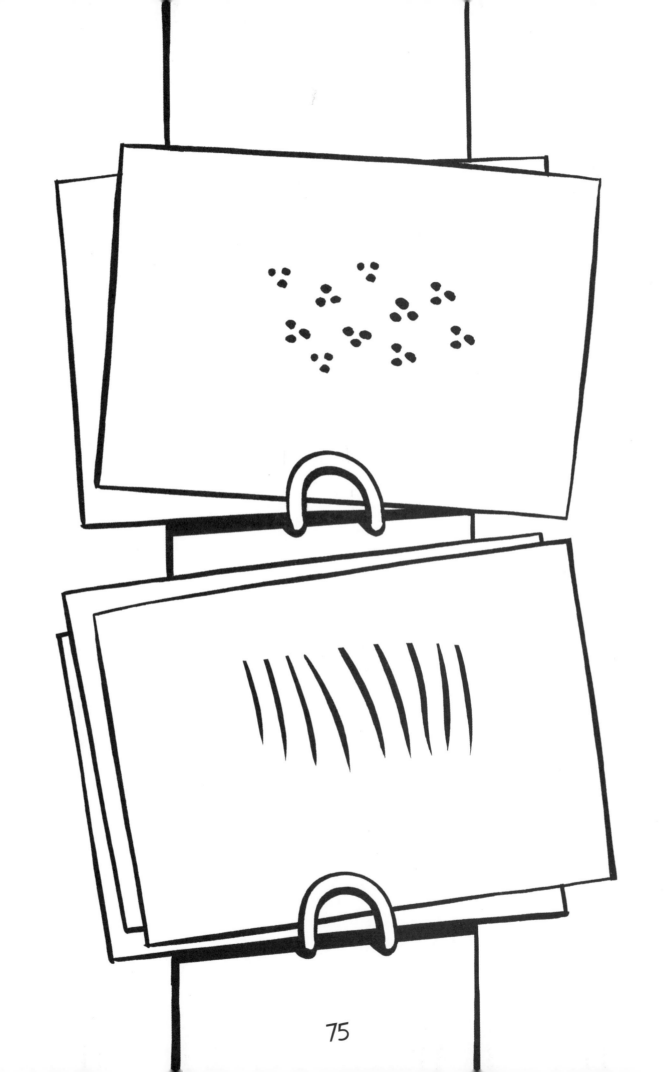

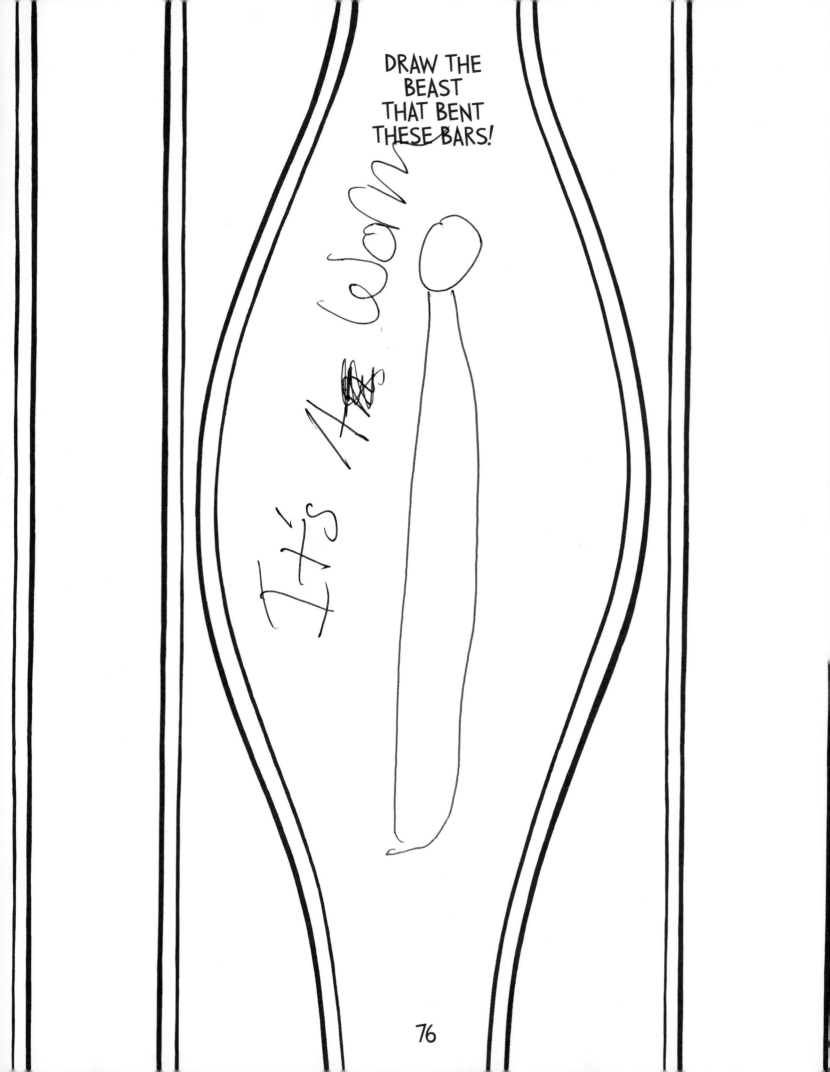

DRAW THE
BEAST
THAT BENT
THESE BARS!

76

SPOT THE 10 DIFFERENCES!

78

TOP SECRET

FACT FILE:

THE
BONSAI
KID

aka
Sidekick
Squirrel

PROFILE:

Strong as a tree, supple as a leaf, thick as a plank.

Trained with Johnny Pecan and Frankie "Nut" Cutlet at the Dodgy Dodo Dojo.

Blackbelt in Martial Farts and Barmi Origami.

Signature fighting move : Flying Nut Butt
Birthstone : Concrete
Favorite motto : No Nuts, No Glory
Weakness : Allergic to folk music

HOW TO DRAW THE BONSAI KID

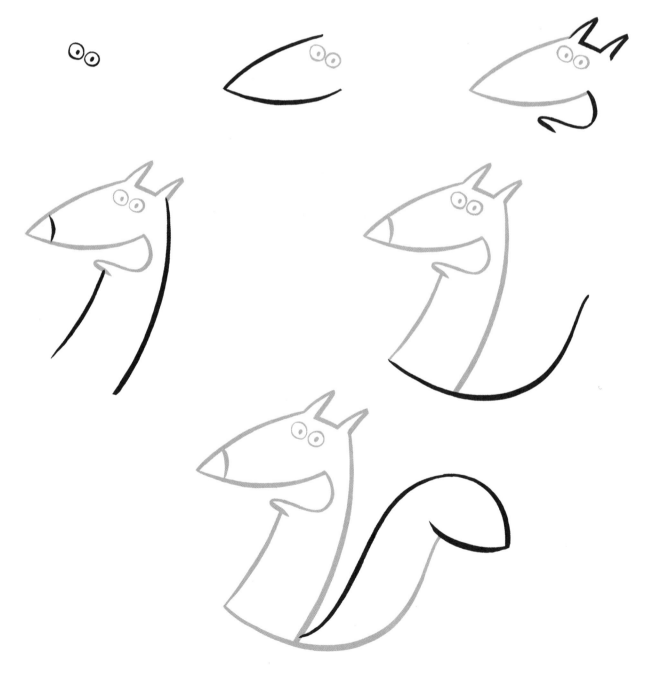

DRAW
YOUR OWN
SIDEKICK
SQUIRREL
HERE!

FILL IN THE
SPEECH BUBBLES

HOW TO DRAW MANIC MONKEYS

DRAW YOUR MANIC MONKEY HERE!

DRAW A PICTURE OF YOUR FAVORITE ANIMAL

THIS IS MY FAVORITE ANIMAL BECAUSE...

DRAW A COMPLETELY NEW SPECIES
NO ONE HAS EVER SEEN BEFORE

HARD

ACROSS
3. THE WORLD'S BIGGEST SNAKE (6)
4. THIS SNAKE LIKES TO ADD UP (5)
6. SNAKES AND VAMPIRES BITE
   WITH THESE (5)
7. ANOTHER NAME FOR SNAKE POISON (5)

DOWN
1. THIS SNAKE LIKES TO SHAKE ITS TAIL (11)
2. DEADLY SNAKE THAT SPITS AT
   ITS VICTIMS (5)
5. THE NOISE A SNAKE MAKES (4)

88

FILL IN THE SQUARES SO THAT EVERY ROW,
EVERY COLUMN, AND EVERY 3X3 BOX
CONTAINS THE NUMBERS 1–9.

DRAW THE ANIMAL
THAT DID THIS DOO-DOO!

WHOSE
BREAKFAST
IS THIS?

91

FAIR

```
F E E D I N G T I M E y
P A D A Z D N P B R A T
Q Q I K O R U O A N R T
P U C D O M D E A E O U
N A E H K H P N T P P N
F R C U E S A I A O M O
V I R G E B R E H S W C
X U E K P W T S Z T S O
Z M A O E B T R F C R C
T H M P R F F L E A P J
S T Y K I A V I A R Y P
Y T L G O N U T A D L J
```

POSTCARD	FLEA
ICE CREAM	TEAPOT
ZOOKEEPER	COCONUT
TYPEWRITER	SHAKESPEARE
AQUARIUM	QUEUE
BANANA	GIFT SHOP
AVIARY	FEEDING TIME

WHICH ANIMAL IS LOSING
ALL ITS HAIR?

CONNECT THE BARNACLES
BENEATH THE BOAT TO
REVEAL AN UNDERWATER
SURPRISE

DRAW A FEARSOME
PIRATE ON DECK

FILL IN THE GAP AND DRAW THE PIRATE CAPTAIN!

99

TOP SECRET

FACT FILE:

CAPTAIN
SCURVY

a.k.a.
The Blue
Rinse Prince

PROFILE:

Lost his leg in Manila,
lost his eye in Bali,
lost his marbles in Romford.

Can kill a man at 20 paces just
by bad breath alone.

World Hopscotch Champion 9
years running.

Signature fighting move : The Rum Punch
Best knot : The Twisted Granny
Favorite cleaning product : Patent Pirate
Parrot Poo Stain Remover

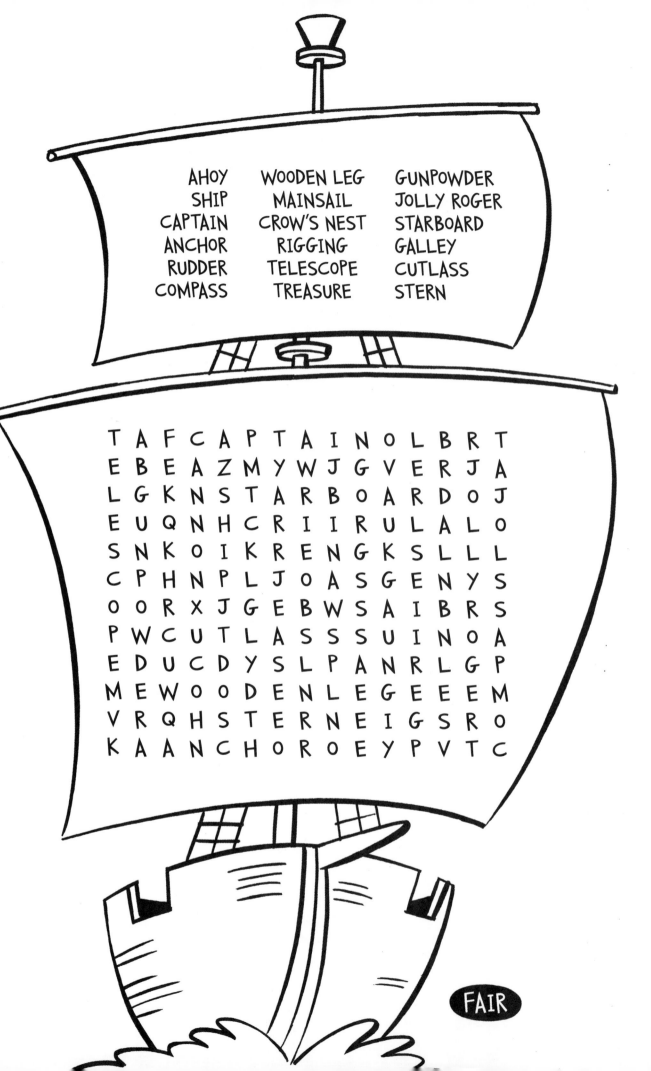

AHOY   WOODEN LEG   GUNPOWDER
SHIP   MAINSAIL   JOLLY ROGER
CAPTAIN   CROW'S NEST   STARBOARD
ANCHOR   RIGGING   GALLEY
RUDDER   TELESCOPE   CUTLASS
COMPASS   TREASURE   STERN

```
T A F C A P T A I N O L B R T
E B E A Z M Y W J G V E R J A
L G K N S T A R B O A R D O J
E U Q N H C R I I R U L A L O
S N K O I K R E N G K S L L L
C P H N P L J O A S G E N Y S
O O R X J G E B W S A I B R S
P W C U T L A S S S U I N O A
E D U C D Y S L P A N R L G P
M E W O O D E N L E G E E E M
V R Q H S T E R N E I G S R O
K A A N C H O R O E Y P V T C
```

FAIR

HOW TO DRAW
A SKULL & CROSSBONES

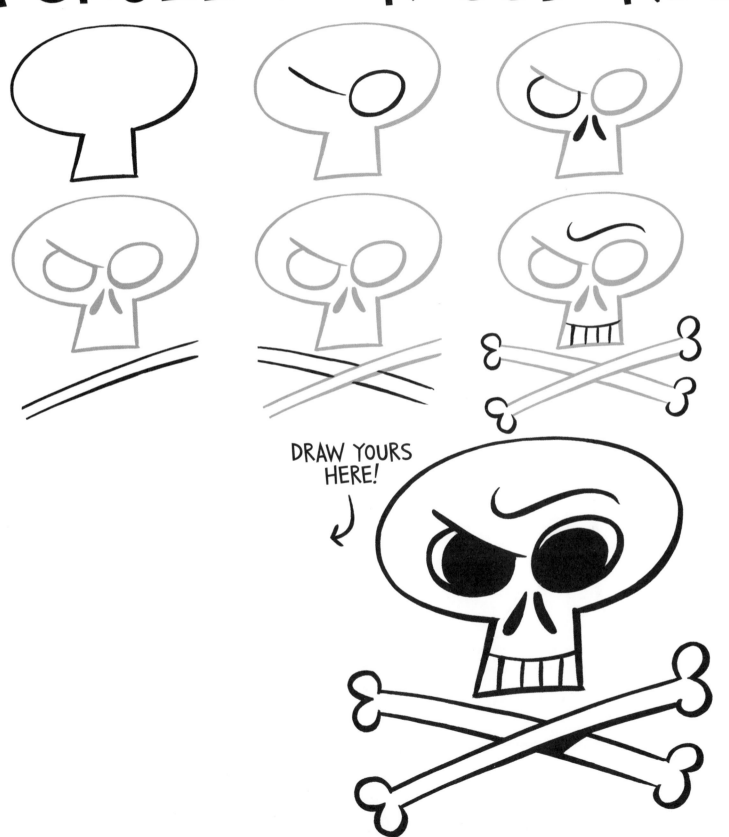

DRAW YOURS HERE!

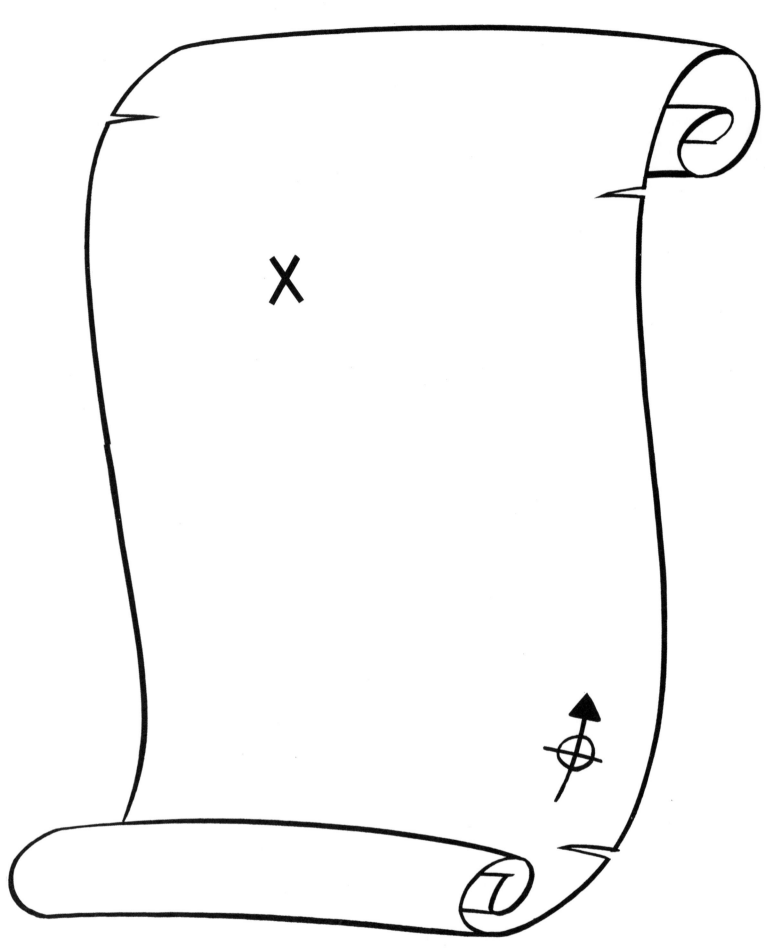

COMPLETE THE PIRATE TREASURE MAP!
(DON'T FORGET THAT "X" MARKS THE SPOT!)

WHAT DOES
CAPTAIN SCURVY
KEEP IN HIS
CHEST?

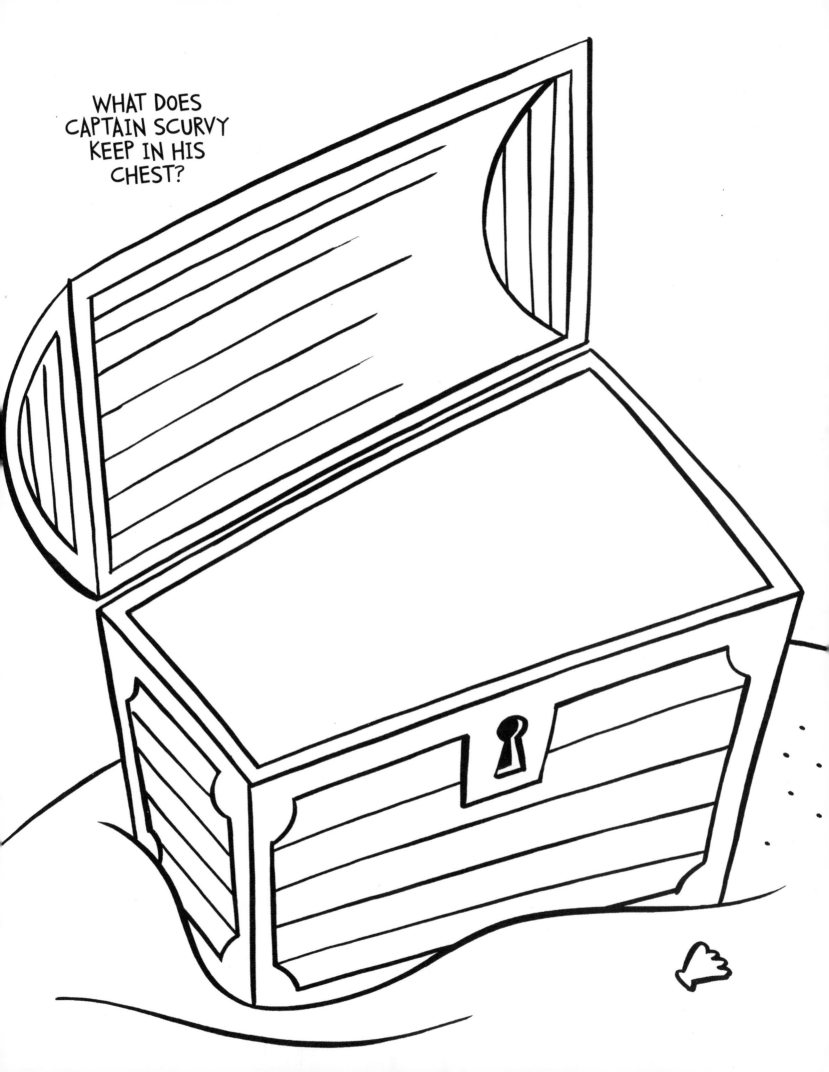

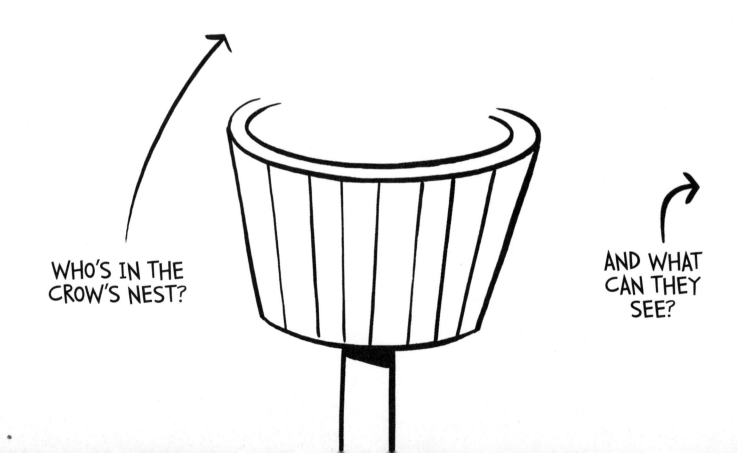

WHO'S IN THE CROW'S NEST?

AND WHAT CAN THEY SEE?

HOW TO DRAW A PIRATE SHIP!

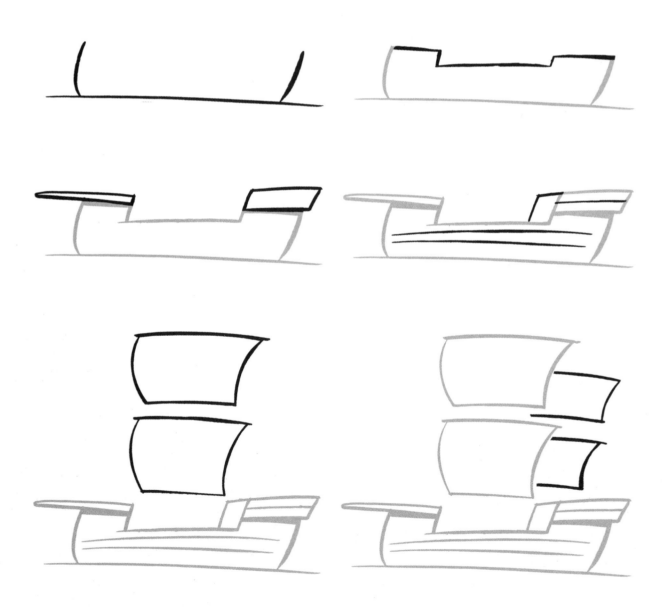

DRAW YOURS HERE!

WHICH PIRATE HAS CAUGHT A FISH?

110

A SURPRISING CATCH!

DRAW THE CONTENTS OF THIS PIRATE'S FISHING BARREL

WHAT CREATURES LIVE IN THIS PIRATE'S BEARD?

SPOT THE 10 DIFFERENCES!

HOW TO DRAW CAPTAIN SCURVY

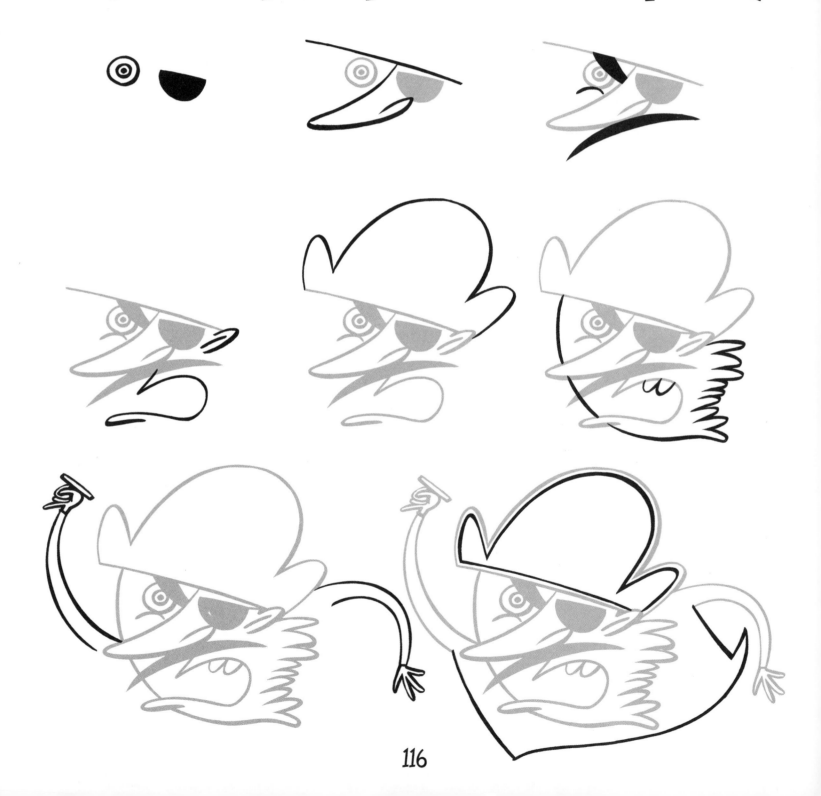

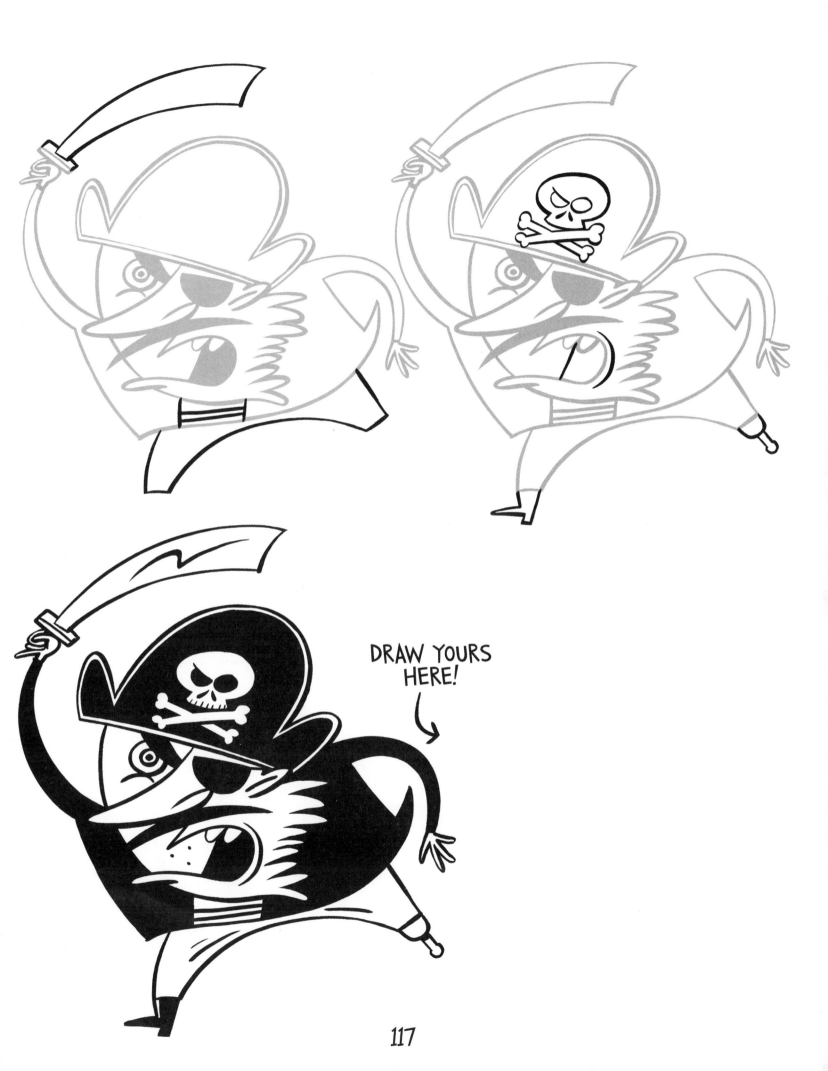

DRAW YOURS HERE!

KOW?

I KNOW THINGS HAVEN'T ALWAYS BEEN EASY FOR US

BUT I JUST WANT YOU TO KNOW THAT WHATEVER HAPPENS NOW...

I'LL ALWAYS THINK OF YOU AS MORE THAN JUST A MOBILE MILK MACHINE

YOU'RE MY SPARRING PARTNER...

MY ROOMMATE...

BUT ABOVE ALL, YOU'RE MY...

...CRAB?!

LOOK ALIVE, ME HEARTIES!

WE WOULDN'T WANT TO KEEP THE SHARKS WAITING FOR THEIR BREAKFAST NOW, WOULD WE?

WAIT! NOT THE LEETLE RAT! I LOVE HEEM!

WHO IS WALKING
THE PLANK
RIGHT NOW?

DRAW THE SEA MONSTER AWAKENED
BY THE BOTTOM BURP OF DOOM!

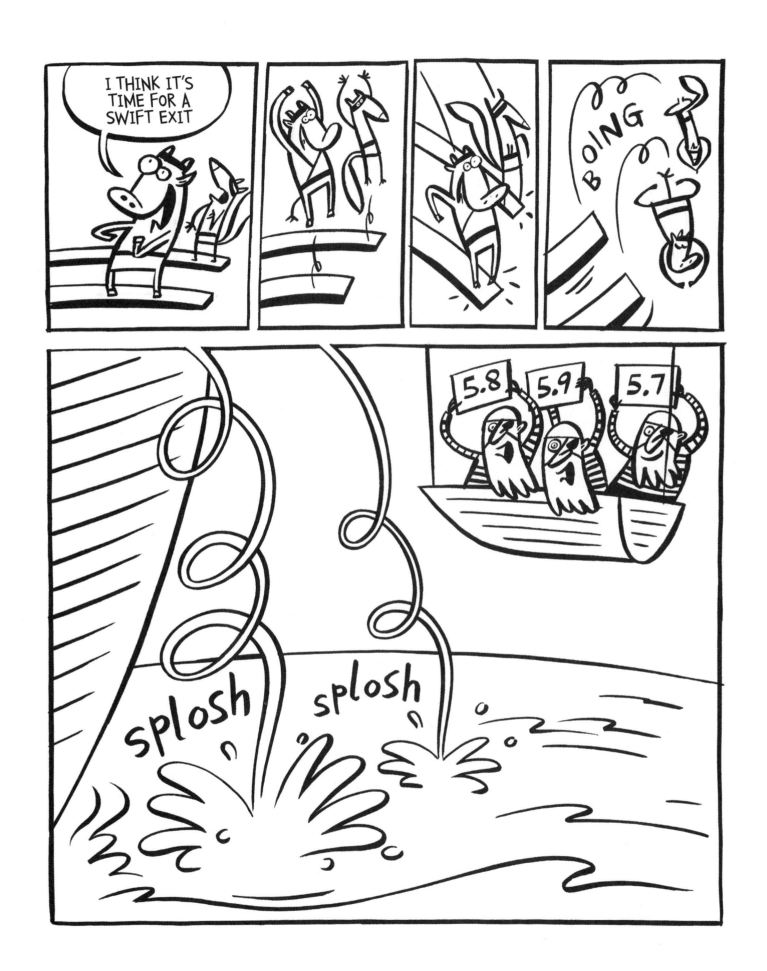

DRAW A DEEP
SEA DIVER!

126

DRAW AN UNDERWATER CITY!

FIND
THAT
NUT!

PLANKTON   SHELL   LIMPET
SHARK   SQUID   DIVER
BLUE WHALE   LOBSTER   CRAB
DOLPHIN   SHIPWRECK SEAWEED

HARD

ACROSS
1. A SPINNING FAN WHICH DRIVES A SHIP (9)
4. THIS BUILDING HELPS SAILORS FIND THEIR WAY AT NIGHT (10)
6. UNDERWATER SHIP (9)
9. CREATURE WITH STINGY TENTACLES (9)
10. PLANK PULLED BY A SPEEDBOAT (8)

DOWN
2. EIGHT LEGS, TWO EYES, ONE UGLY TEMPER (7)
3. ANOTHER NAME FOR WHALE FAT (7)
5. TUBE FOR BREATHING UNDERWATER (7)
7. HALF WOMAN, HALF FISH (7)
8. GEM SOMETIMES FOUND IN OYSTER SHELLS (5)

FAIR

WHAT ARE THESE
WORMS TALKING
ABOUT?

WHICH CREATURE
IS MAKING
ALL THESE
BUBBLES?

WHAT DID THIS SHARK
HAVE FOR DINNER?

WHAT IS THIS CRAB
HOLDING IN ITS CLAW?

TOP SECRET

FACT FILE:

MUTANT
MERMAID

a.k.a.
The Toxic
Terror

PROFILE:

Half woman, half fish, all mutant!
Mother is a nurse, father is a
sturgeon.
Acquired mutant powers after
eating a radioactive fish finger.

Signature fighting move : The Caviar Crunch
Place of birth : Cape Cod
Favorite song : Mad About The Buoy
Favorite food : Lighthouse keepers

HOW TO DRAW MUTANT MERMAID

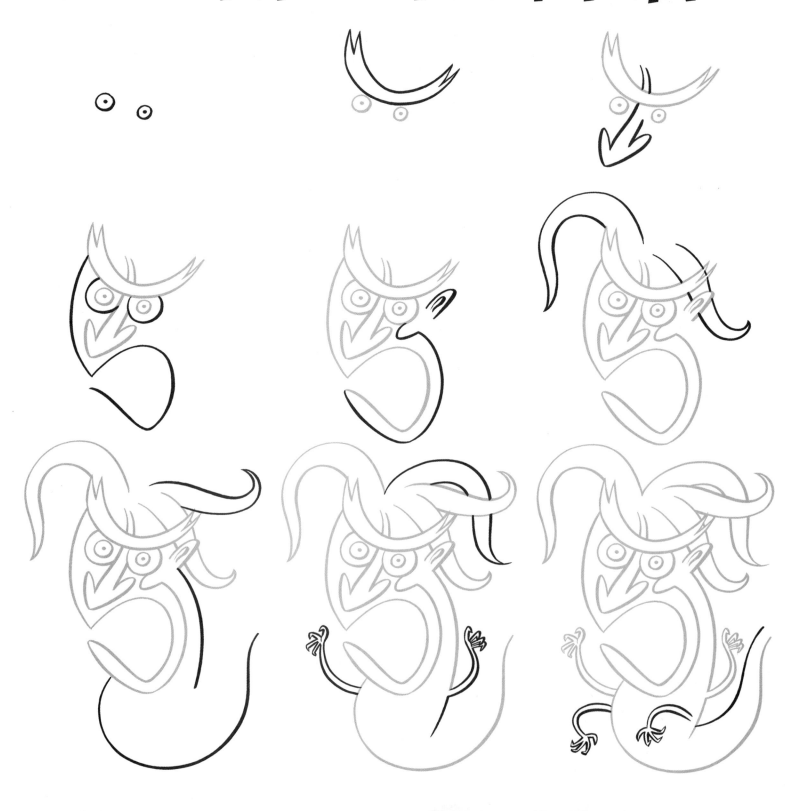

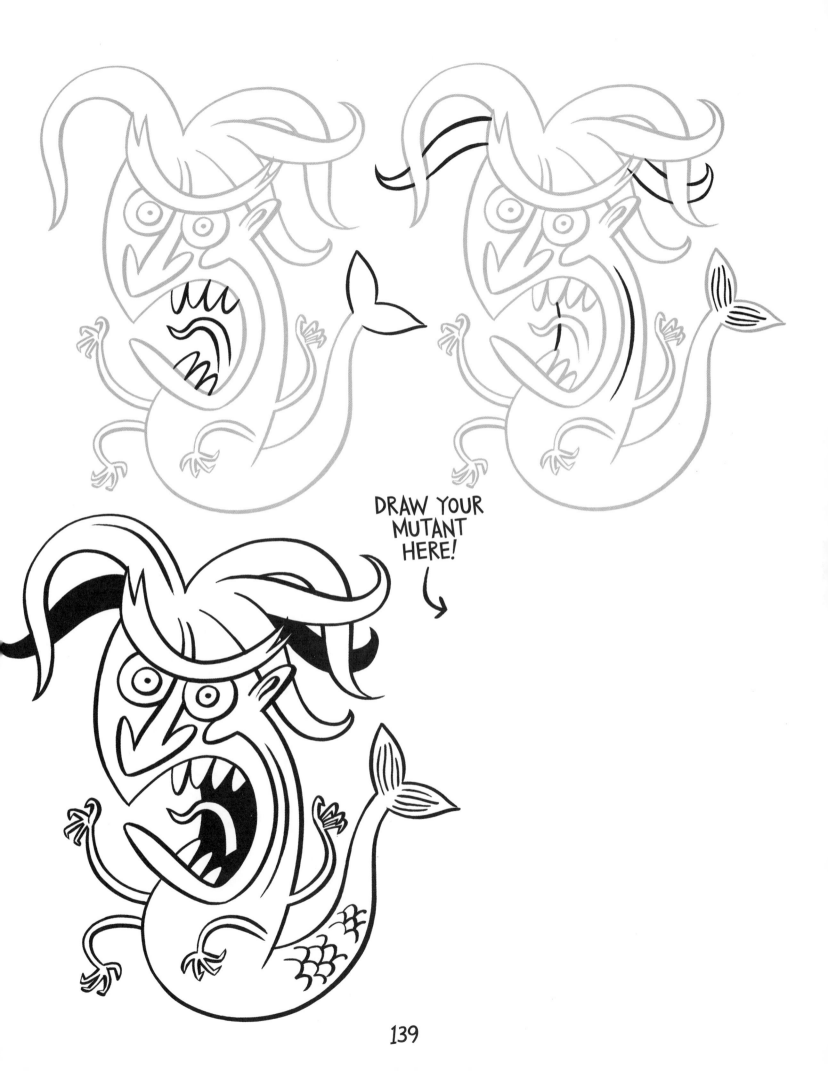

DRAW YOUR MUTANT HERE!

NOW MAKE UP YOUR OWN
MUTANT MERMAID!

INTERMISSION

TIME TO PUT ON YOUR PENCILS AND SHARPEN YOUR THINKING CAPS!

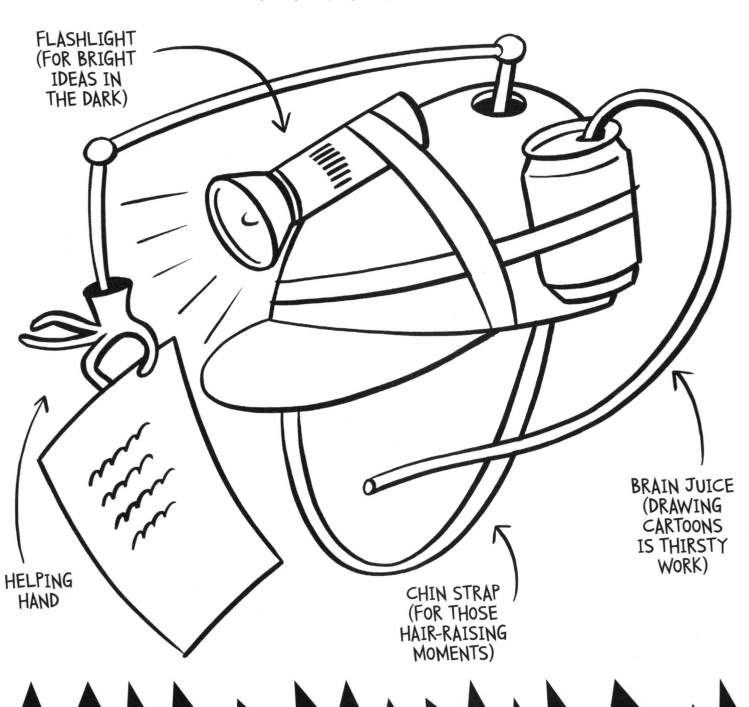

FLASHLIGHT
(FOR BRIGHT
IDEAS IN
THE DARK)

HELPING
HAND

CHIN STRAP
(FOR THOSE
HAIR-RAISING
MOMENTS)

BRAIN JUICE
(DRAWING
CARTOONS
IS THIRSTY
WORK)

AS WE'RE UNDERWATER,
LET'S LOOK AT
BUBBLES!

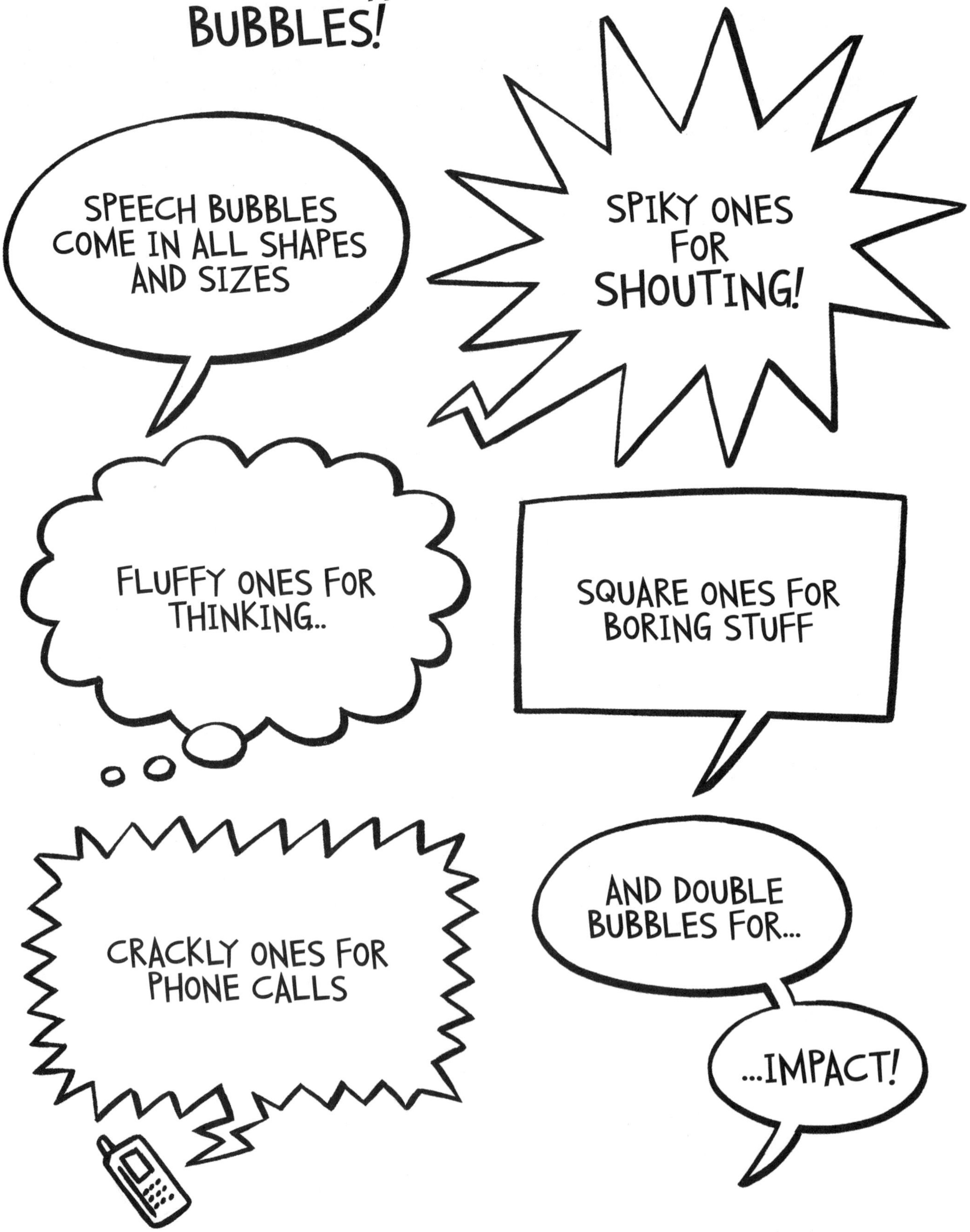

WHAT ARE THEY SAYING?
DRAW BUBBLES FOR THESE CHARACTERS.

THESE FISH ARE
HIDING IN THE SAND.
CAN YOU SEE WHAT
THEY LOOK LIKE?

FILL IN THIS SPEECH BUBBLE!

HOW TO DRAW OCTAVIUS PLOK

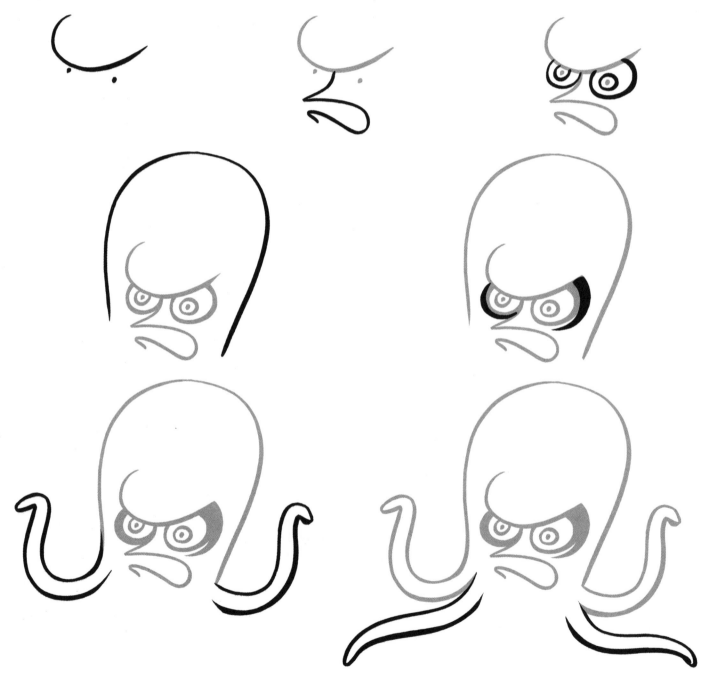

DRAW YOUR
EIGHT-LEGGED
FIEND HERE!

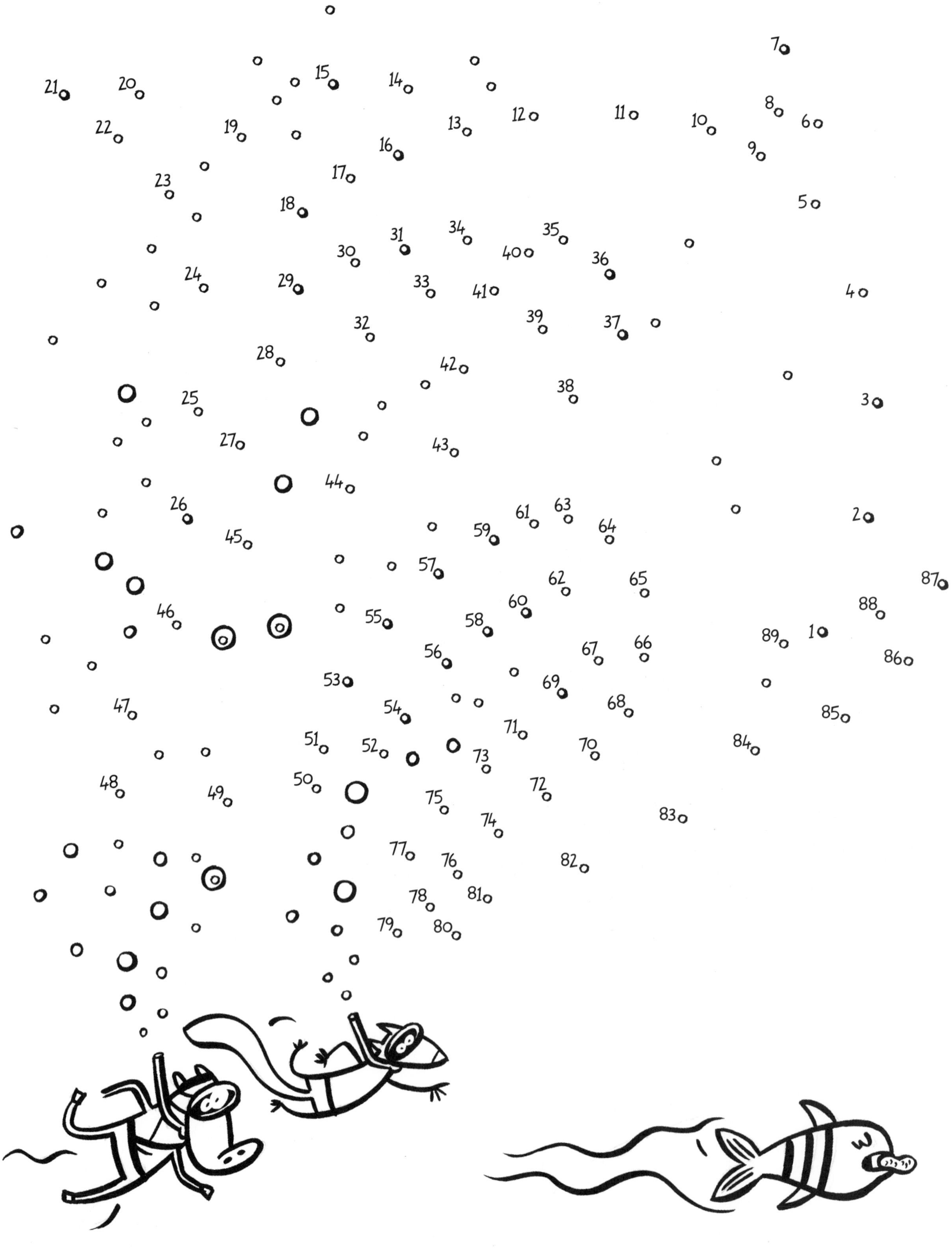
1
2
3
4
5
6
7
8
9
10
11
12
13
14
15
16
17
18
19
20
21
22
23
24
25
26
27
28
29
30
31
32
33
34
35
36
37
38
39
40
41
42
43
44
45
46
47
48
49
50
51
52
53
54
55
56
57
58
59
60
61
62
63
64
65
66
67
68
69
70
71
72
73
74
75
76
77
78
79
80
81
82
83
84
85
86
87
88
89

WHAT ARE THESE FISH SWIMMING AWAY FROM?

LOOK! HE'S SLOWING DOWN

CL-UNK

ACK ACK

KA-PLONK! KA-PLUNK!

KA-PUT

HMM... THIS FISH SEEMS A LITTLE, ER... FISHY

OR NOT! LOOK!

YOU REALIZE WHAT THIS MEANS?

ROBOCOD MADE IN FIN-LAND

MUTANT MERMAID'S UNCLE IS A ROBOT?

THINK ABOUT IT— A ROBOT FISH, A PIRATE PARROT...

POP!

WE NEED TO GET TO THE BOTTOM OF THIS RIGHT...

YOW!

WHO HARPOONED WHO?

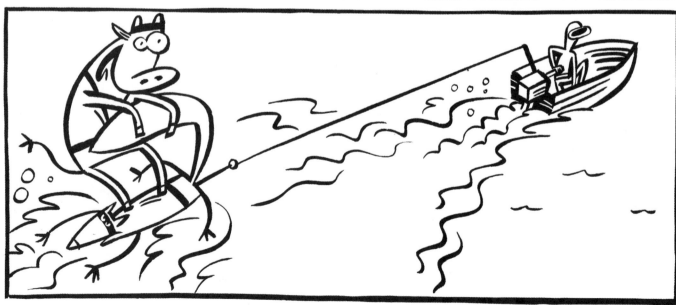

HOW TO DRAW A CREEPY CASTLE

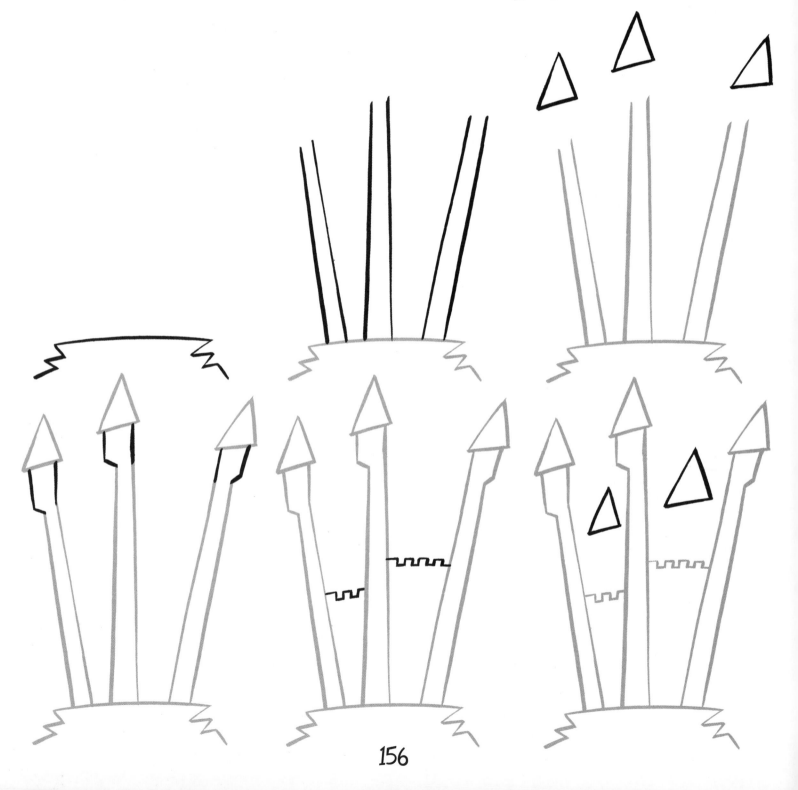

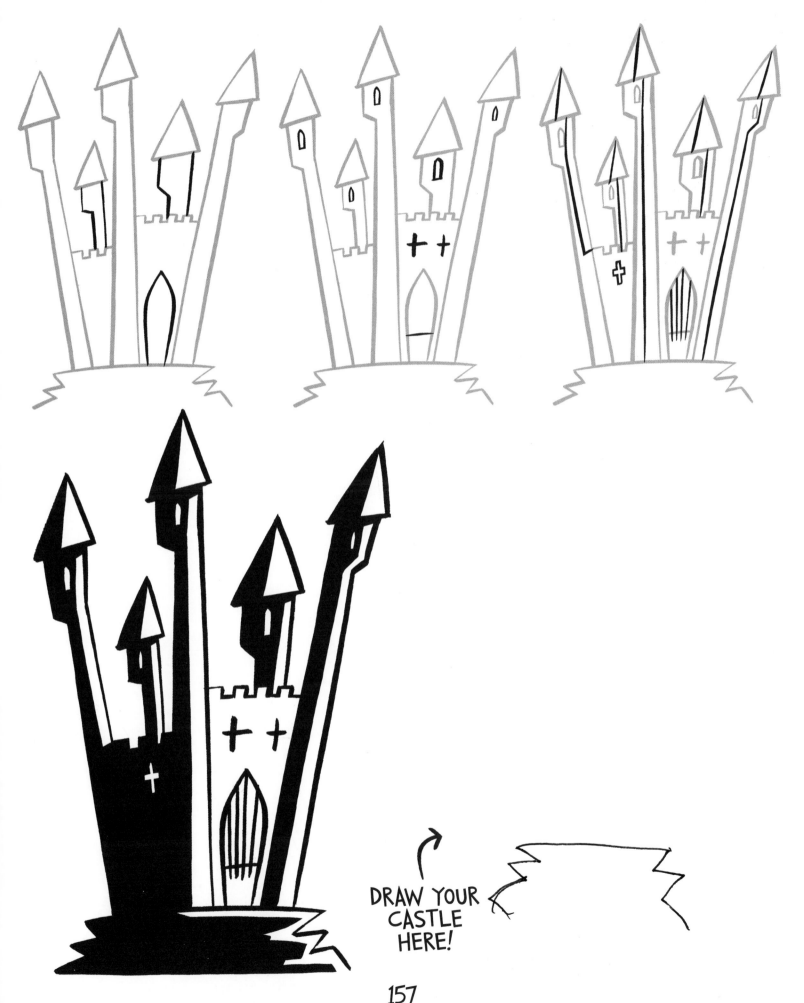

DRAW YOUR CASTLE HERE!

SPOT
THE 10
DIFFERENCES!

ACROSS
2. A WITCH MIGHT FLY ON THIS (10)
7. THE MOST FAMOUS VAMPIRE OF ALL (7)
8. FOREST PERSON WITH POINTY EARS (3)
9. GHOSTS CAN PASS THROUGH THESE (5)
11. A SPIDER SPINS THIS (3)
12. PRISONERS RATTLE THESE (6)
13. WHERE PRISONERS ARE KEPT (7)

DOWN
1. LOWER THIS TO PROTECT A CASTLE (10)
3. WATER AROUND A CASTLE (4)
4. TALLEST PART OF A CASTLE (5)
5. A VAMPIRE SLEEPS IN ONE OF THESE (6)
6. RAISE THIS TO PROTECT A CASTLE (10)
10. DRIVE THIS THROUGH A VAMPIRE'S HEART TO KILL HIM (5)

FAIR

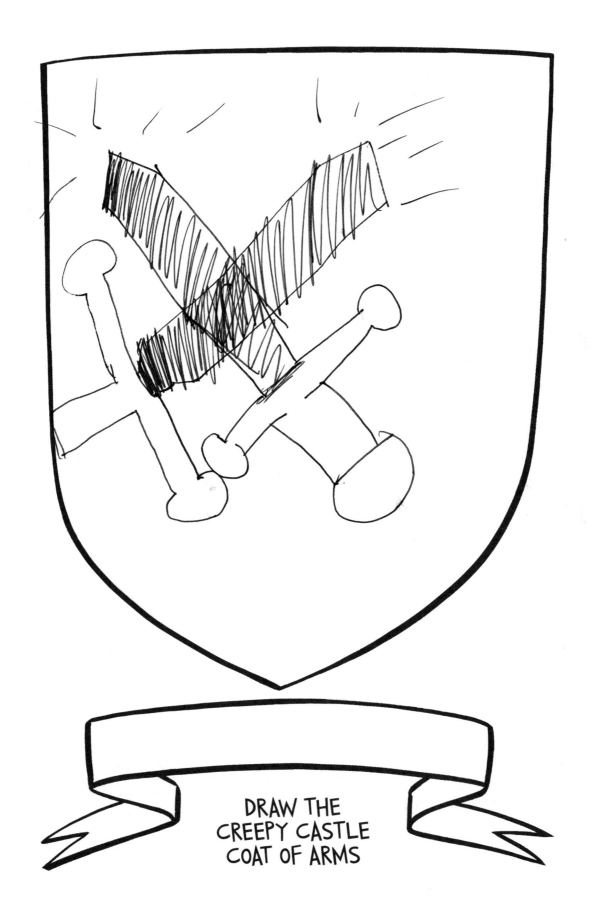

DRAW THE
CREEPY CASTLE
COAT OF ARMS

COMPLETE
THESE
CREEPY
PORTRAITS

COUNT SCROFULA

LORD MISHMASH

HOW TO DRAW A VAMPIRE BAT

DRAW YOUR BATTY PICTURE HERE!

FIND YOUR WAY
THROUGH IGOR'S
BRAIN

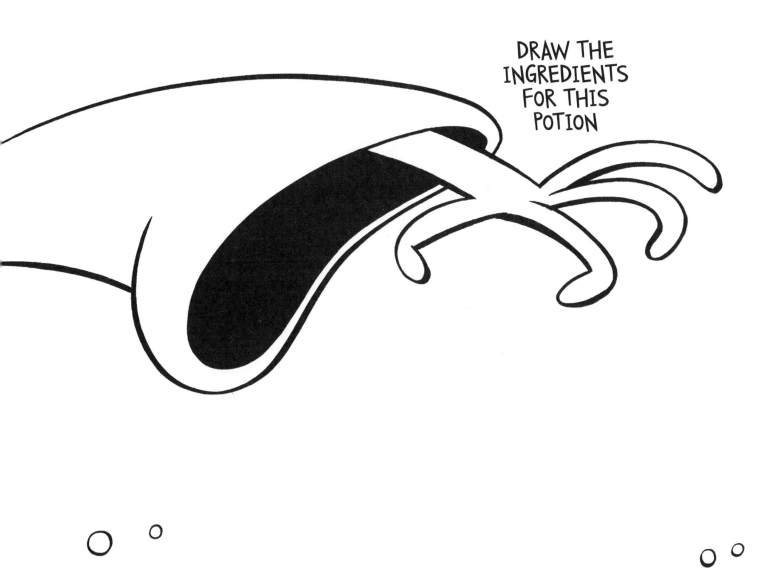

DRAW
A WIZARD!

DRAW
A WICKED
WITCH!

My Spell

My spell sets fire to any thin in 5 miles around it, every thing except every thing

WRITE A SPELL!

WHAT HAPPENS WHEN YOU
CAST YOUR SPELL?

People Die

FILL IN THE
SQUARES SO EVERY
ROW, COLUMN, AND
2x2 BOX
CONTAINS THE
NUMBERS 1-4.

EASY

UNTANGLE THESE PRISONERS' BEARDS
TO FIND THE KEY AND SET THEM FREE.

DRAW THE MONSTER CHAINED
IN THE FORGOTTEN DUNGEON

177

SPOT THE 10 DIFFERENCES!

HOW TO DRAW BOOGIE KNIGHT

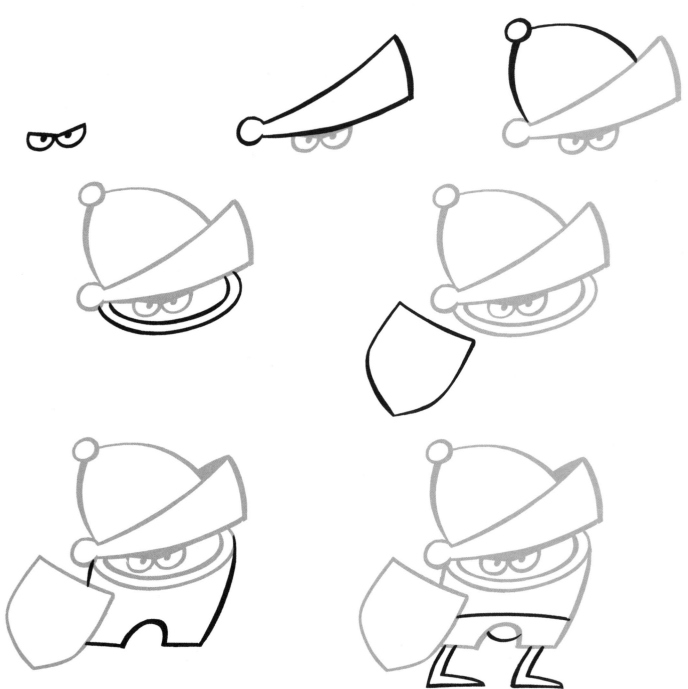

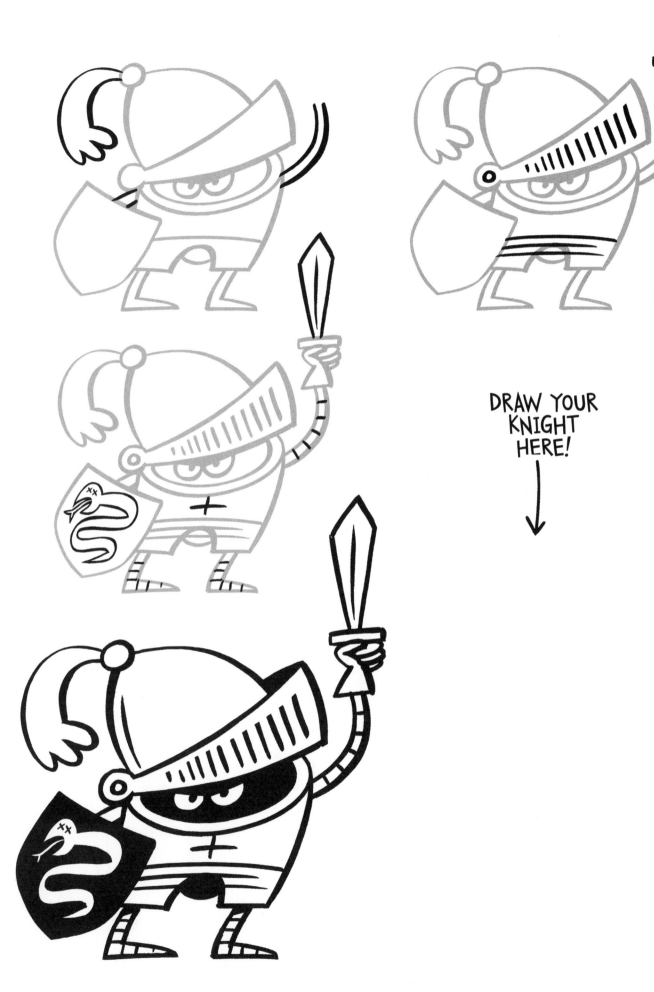

DRAW YOUR
KNIGHT
HERE!

```
Z N H S V U D F K N W Z
L I L T P I L A E R G O
R E T S N O M T C L R M
H T R I W I L R B Y E B
F S E E T I P C T F M I
T N R G Y Y T S Y D L E
I E E R F M O C R C I R
W K C E O H M A H L N I
C N R T G T G U M Y P P
O A O L R O G Y M C N M
F R S O N I L B O G Y A
W F L P D Z I M V E U V
```

ZOMBIE	WEREWOLF	OGRE
CYCLOPS	POLTERGEIST	VAMPIRE
DRAGON	MONSTER	WITCH
GHOST	SORCERER	GREMLIN
GOBLIN	FRANKENSTEIN	MUMMY

HARD

SUPERHERO CITY

CAN YOU FIND YOUR WAY
THROUGH THE SUPER CITY STREETS?

ACROSS
3. THIS ROAD LEADS NOWHERE (4,3)
6. KEEPS YOUR MONEY SAFE (4)
7. WATCH FILMS HERE (6)
8. MOVING STAIRCASE (9)
9. WHERE PLANES LAND (7)

FAIR

DOWN
1. WHERE SUPERHEROES DO THEIR SHOPPING (11)
2. BORROW BOOKS FROM HERE (7)
4. VERY TALL BUILDING (10)
5. UNDERGROUND TUNNEL FULL OF POO (5)

BECOME A SUPERHERO!

1. WHAT IS YOUR SUPERHERO NAME?

Dodo everything

2. WHAT IS YOUR SUPERPOWER?

all

3. HOW DID YOU GET IT?

born with it

4. WHAT COLOR IS YOUR SUPER COSTUME?

red and Black

5. DO YOU WEAR YOUR PANTS ON THE INSIDE OR OUTSIDE?

NOW INVENT YOUR SUPERHERO
SECRET IDENTITY!

6. MAKE UP AN UNDERCOVER NAME

BOB

7. WHAT IS YOUR DAY JOB?

eletritton

8. WHERE DO YOU WORK?

every where

9. WHAT CLOTHES DO YOU WEAR?

safty stuff

10. WHERE DO YOU GO TO CHANGE INTO
YOUR SUPERHERO COSTUME?

some where were
no one is

MATCH THESE SUPERHEROES TO THEIR SECRET IDENTITIES

MYSTERY GIRL

GINGER NINJA

DR. X-RAY

BURGER BOY

RADIOACTIVE RABBIT

CAPTAIN DISASTER

CHARLIE
PORK

REGGIE
BONK

ELOISE
GUPPY

PETER
PERK

HAROLD
HARPER

XAVIER
STRONG

DRAW THE SUPERHERO
LIFTING THIS CAR
IN THE AIR

DRAW THE REST OF THIS
MASKED SUPERHERO

NEW HERO IN TOWN

IF YOU WERE A SUPERHERO,
WHAT WOULD YOU LOOK LIKE?

DRAW YOURSELF PERFORMING
A SUPERHERO FEAT!

WHAT DOES THE PAPER
SAY ABOUT WHAT YOU DID?

THE CITY GIVES YOU AN AWARD -
WHAT DOES IT LOOK LIKE?

SUPERHERO
OF THE
MONTH

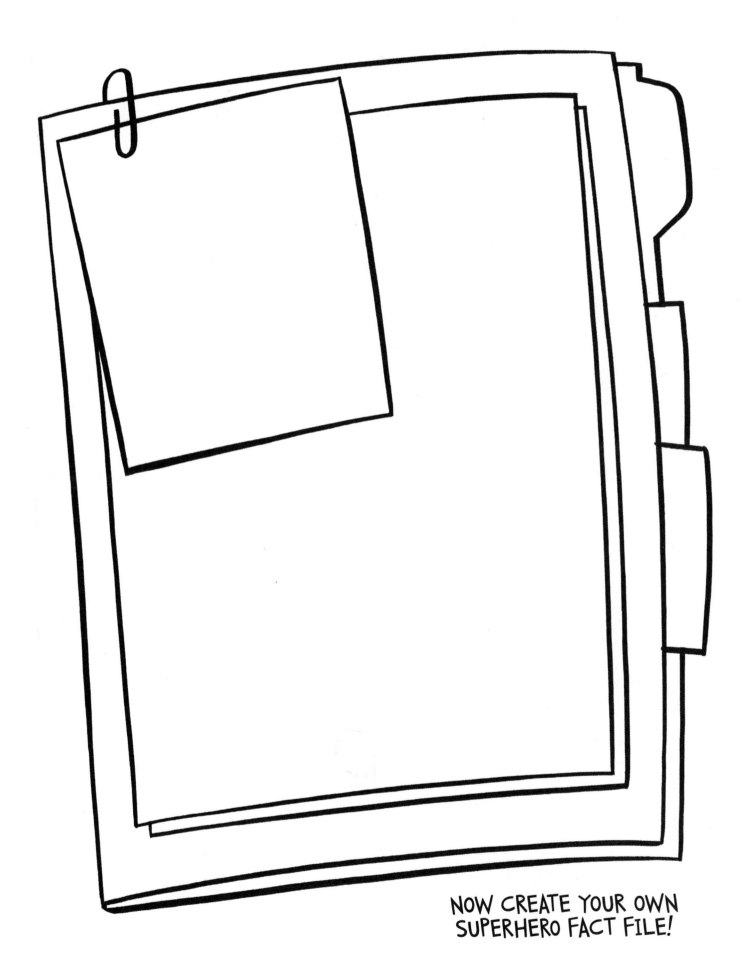

NOW CREATE YOUR OWN
SUPERHERO FACT FILE!

CAN YOU FIND 10 DIFFERENCES BETWEEN THESE PICTURES?

SOMEONE HAS
SMASHED THIS
PRICELESS STATUE.
WHAT DID IT
LOOK LIKE?

HARD

ACROSS

6. SALE OF ART TO THE HIGHEST BIDDER (7)
7. OLD BONE OR PREHISTORIC RELIC (6)
8. PLACE WHERE ARTISTS EXHIBIT (7)

DOWN

1. PICTURE IN A FRAME MADE WITH A BRUSH (8)
2. VERY FAMOUS ARTIST, FIRST NAME PABLO (7)
3. CUT HIS EAR OFF AND PAINTED SUNFLOWERS (3,4)
4. PORTRAIT WITH THE MYSTERIOUS SMILE (4,4)
5. ARTISTS CARVE THESE OUT OF WOOD, CLAY (9)

204

CAN YOU CRACK THE CODE TO THE MUSEUM SAFE?

2, 4, 8, 16, __

1, 8, 15, 22, __

3, 5, 9, 17, __

4, 6, 9, 13, __

WHAT'S
INSIDE?

SOMEONE HAS STOLEN THE WORLD'S MOST EXPENSIVE PAINTING

BY VINCENT VAN DRIVER

CAN YOU REPLACE IT?

MAKE SURE EVERY ROW, COLUMN, AND 2X2 BOX CONTAINS THE NUMBERS 1-4.

TOP SECRET

FACT FILE:

SUPERCOOT

aka
The Wigless
Wonder

PROFILE:

Fast as a rocket, strong as an ox,
bald as a baby.

Lost his hair aged 6 after a freak
porridge accident.

Winner of the Best Earwax Sculpture
prize five years in a row.

Nonsuper alter ego : Jimmy Pepper
Archenemy : Wigzilla
Signature fighting move : Shampoo Shimmy
Motto : Hair Today, Gone Tomorrow

HOW TO DRAW SUPERCOOT

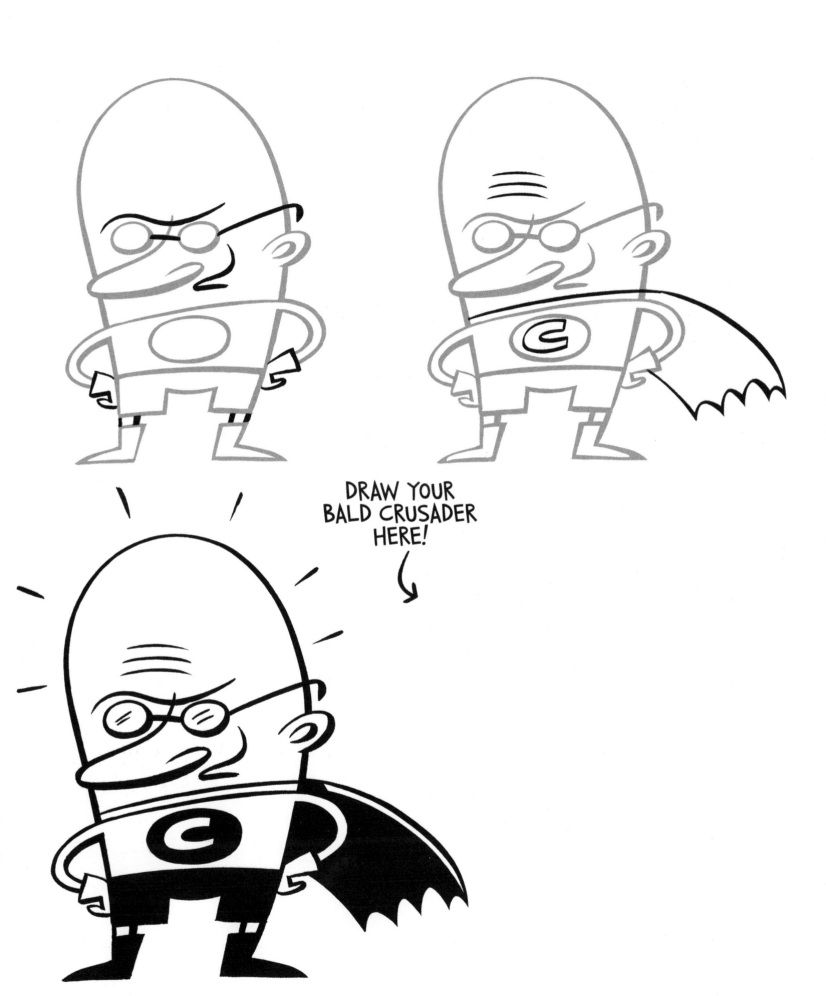

DRAW YOUR
BALD CRUSADER
HERE!

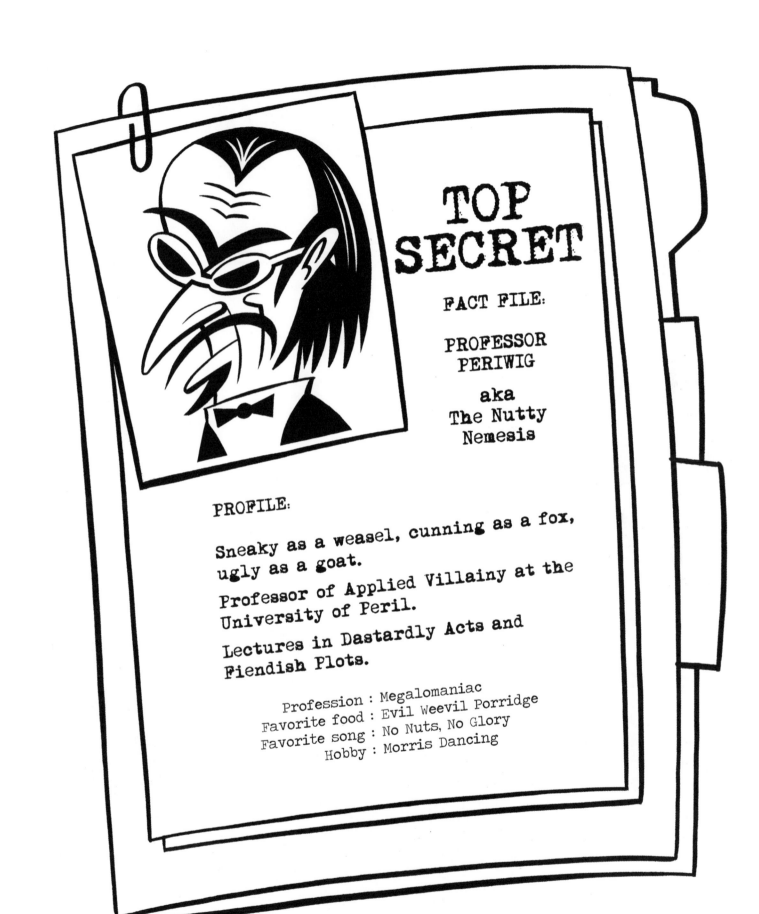

TOP
SECRET

FACT FILE:

PROFESSOR
PERIWIG

aka
The Nutty
Nemesis

PROFILE:

Sneaky as a weasel, cunning as a fox,
ugly as a goat.

Professor of Applied Villainy at the
University of Peril.

Lectures in Dastardly Acts and
Fiendish Plots.

Profession : Megalomaniac
Favorite food : Evil Weevil Porridge
Favorite song : No Nuts, No Glory
Hobby : Morris Dancing

SPOT THE DIFFERENCE!

CAN YOU SPOT THE 10 DIFFERENCES
BETWEEN THESE TWO PICTURES?

QUICK! DRAW A CRAZY CAR FOR KOW KAPOW
SO HE CAN SET OFF IN HOT PURSUIT.

AND NOW DRAW A VIRTUAL VEHICLE
FOR THE BONSAI KID

NOW DESIGN A CRAZY CAR FOR YOU TO DRIVE

NOW DESIGN A CRAZY CAR FOR YOU TO DRIVE

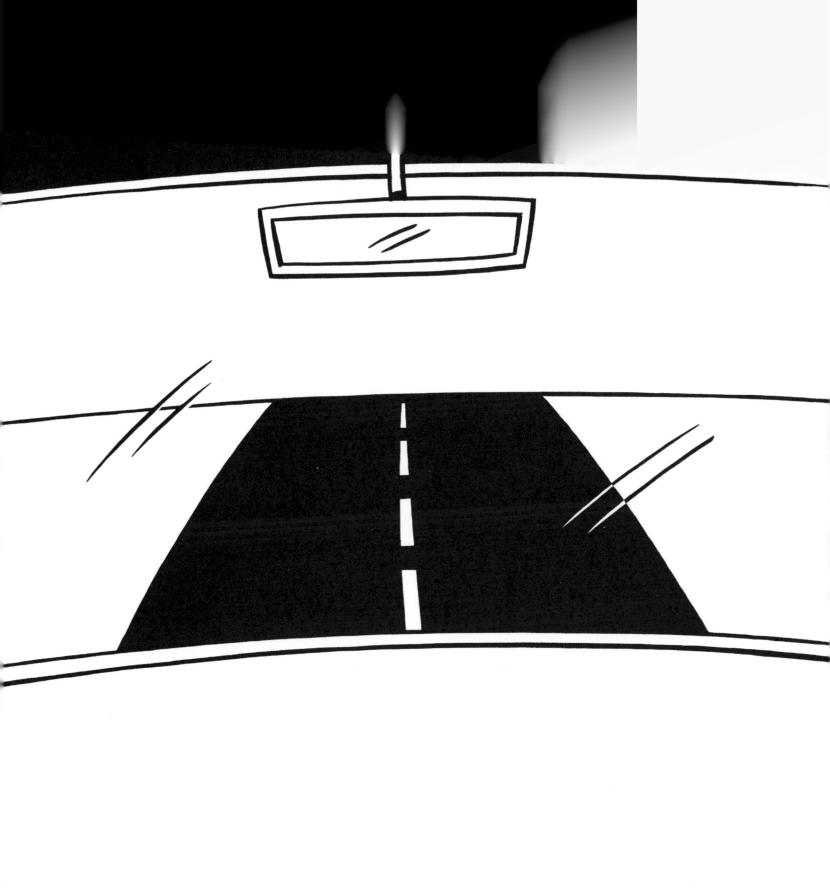

SOUPED UP! DESIGN A
CAR THAT RUNS ON
TOMATO SOUP
INSTEAD OF GAS!

224

PUT YOURSELF
INSIDE THIS
CRASH HELMET

225

```
R C I S H O N G K O N G L B T S
C G R A N O O A O N R M N P I E
G P T K Z C D H I K O S H R U I
A A E M O R N O R R J C A S B L
U R R L O E O K I O O P N H U A
K I T D N S L A E Y C B O J T L
D I S N U Y C S J W L G I R K I
A O U N E B N O P E U O A B U N
L H S N J E L J W N P K M Y B A
L B D L H U M I O K A M U W M M
A Y D T O K Y O N J C R T A I O
S W A W M O N T R E A L W U T P
```

HARD

ROME   CAIRO
PARIS   HANOI
LONDON   NAIROBI
ATHENS   MOSCOW
DALLAS   NEW YORK   ACAPULCO
DUBLIN   OSLO   TIMBUKTU
MANILA   TOKYO   SYDNEY
JAKARTA   MONTREAL   HONG KONG

226

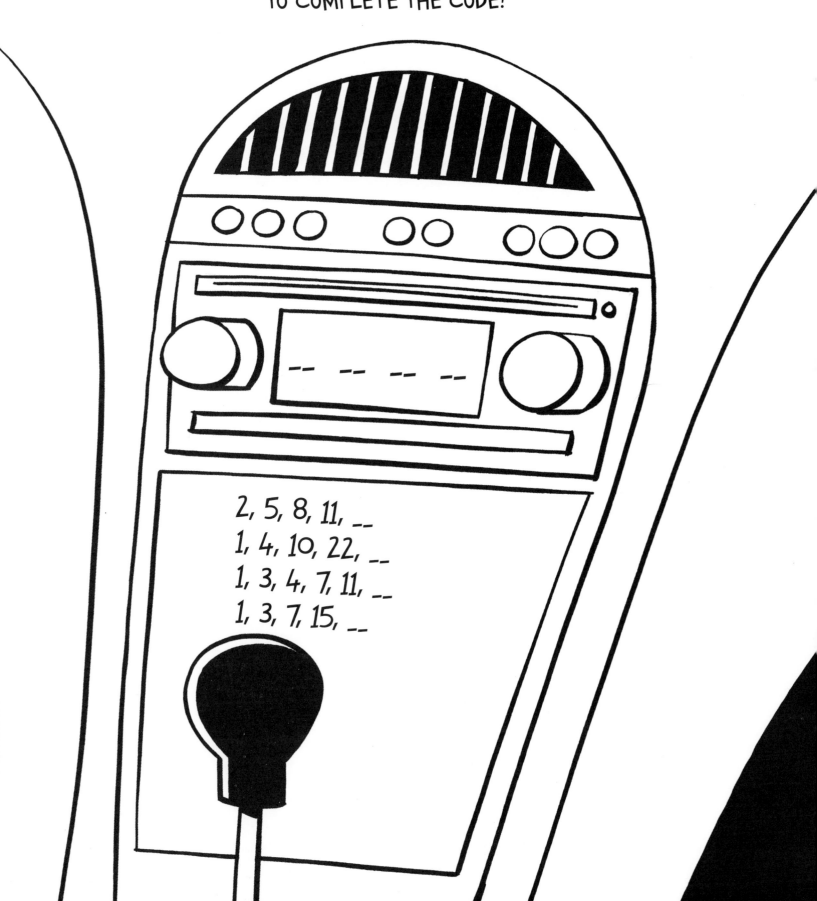

THE RADIO WON'T WORK!
CAN YOU FIND THE MISSING NUMBERS
TO COMPLETE THE CODE?

2, 5, 8, 11, __
1, 4, 10, 22, __
1, 3, 4, 7, 11, __
1, 3, 7, 15, __

HOW TO DRAW A RACING CAR

DRAW YOUR
CAR HERE!

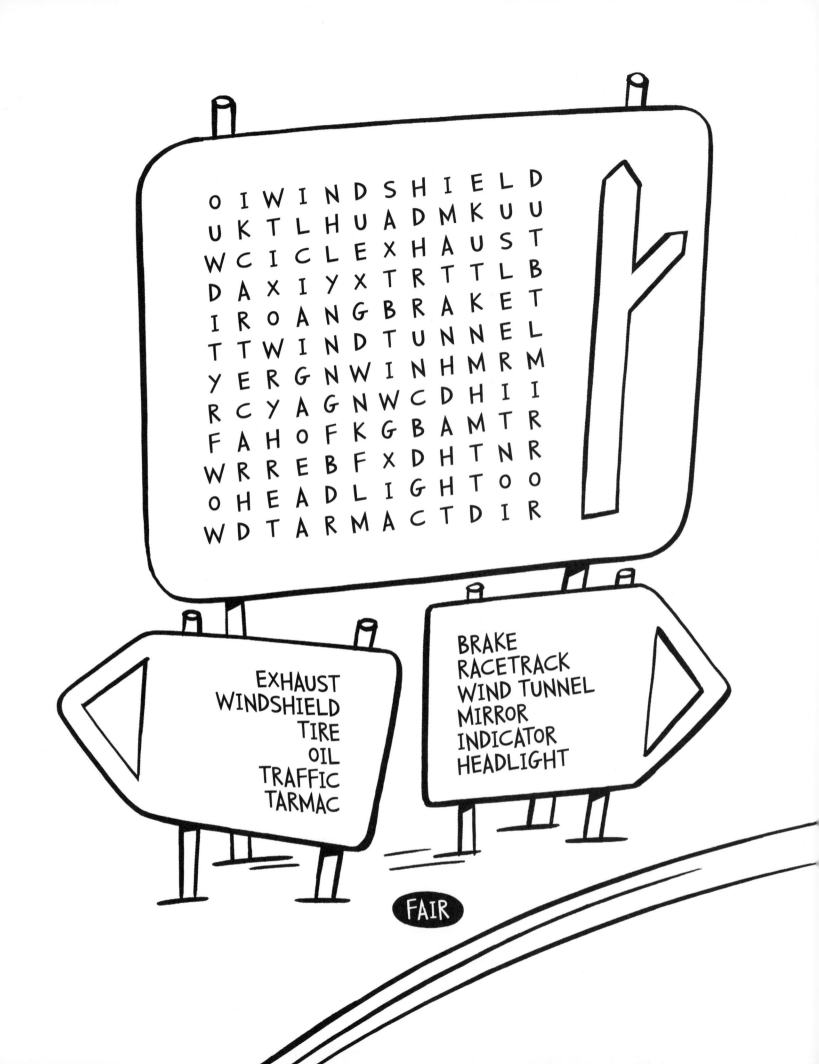

ACROSS
3. SOMEONE WHO FIXES ENGINES (8)
5. GO PAST ANOTHER CAR (8)
9. CHANGE TIRES AND REFUEL HERE (3)
10. THE PERSON AT THE WHEEL (6)
11. BRITISH WORD FOR WHAT YOU PUT IN YOUR TANK (6)
13. THE MOST IMPORTANT PART OF THE CAR (6)

DOWN
1. SHOWS HOW FAST YOU'RE GOING (11)
2. BEND THAT GOES BACK ON ITSELF (7)
4. CHANGE THESE TO GO FASTER (5)
7. USE THESE TO STOP (6)
8. THIS PROTECTS YOUR HEAD (6)
12. ONCE AROUND THE CIRCUIT (3)

HARD

LET'S DRAW THE LOUDEST COMIC IN THE WORLD!

WHERE ARE PLACES WITH PLENTY OF NOISE?

WHAT ACTIVITIES MAKE LOTS OF SOUNDS?

WRITE YOUR IDEAS HERE

GO FOR IT!

NOW PUT YOURSELF IN THE HOT SEAT FOR THE

CRAZY QUIZ!

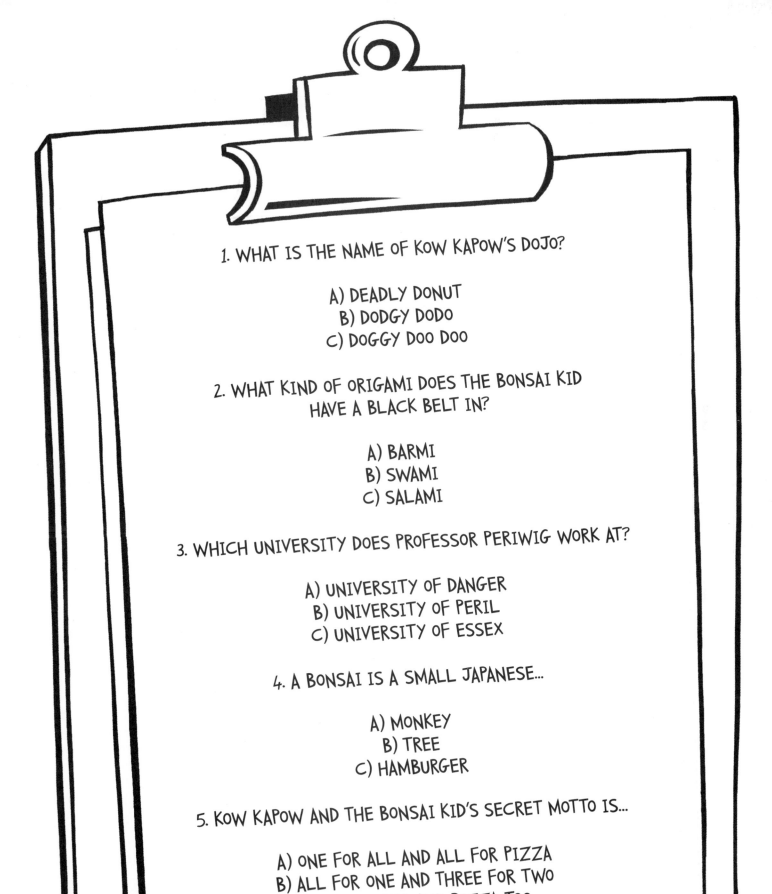

1. WHAT IS THE NAME OF KOW KAPOW'S DOJO?

    A) DEADLY DONUT
    B) DODGY DODO
    C) DOGGY DOO DOO

2. WHAT KIND OF ORIGAMI DOES THE BONSAI KID
HAVE A BLACK BELT IN?

    A) BARMI
    B) SWAMI
    C) SALAMI

3. WHICH UNIVERSITY DOES PROFESSOR PERIWIG WORK AT?

    A) UNIVERSITY OF DANGER
    B) UNIVERSITY OF PERIL
    C) UNIVERSITY OF ESSEX

4. A BONSAI IS A SMALL JAPANESE...

    A) MONKEY
    B) TREE
    C) HAMBURGER

5. KOW KAPOW AND THE BONSAI KID'S SECRET MOTTO IS...

    A) ONE FOR ALL AND ALL FOR PIZZA
    B) ALL FOR ONE AND THREE FOR TWO
    C) AWFUL TEA AND PIZZA TOO

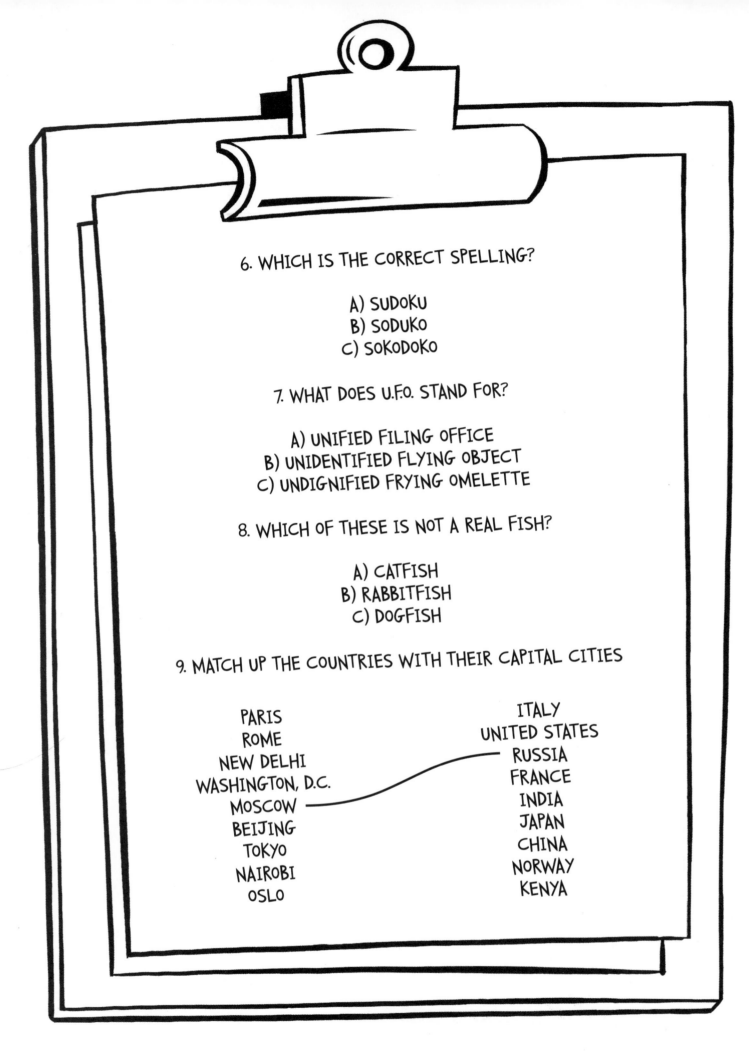

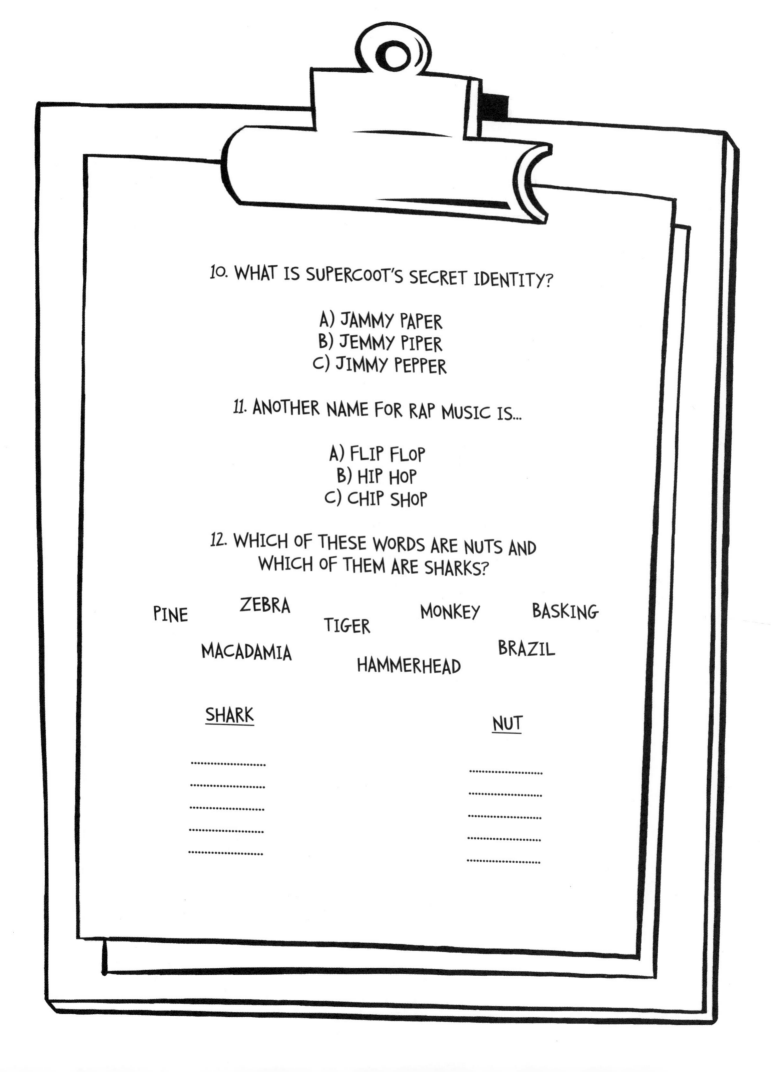

10. WHAT IS SUPERCOOT'S SECRET IDENTITY?

A) JAMMY PAPER
B) JEMMY PIPER
C) JIMMY PEPPER

11. ANOTHER NAME FOR RAP MUSIC IS...

A) FLIP FLOP
B) HIP HOP
C) CHIP SHOP

12. WHICH OF THESE WORDS ARE NUTS AND WHICH OF THEM ARE SHARKS?

PINE   ZEBRA   MONKEY   BASKING

TIGER

MACADAMIA   HAMMERHEAD   BRAZIL

SHARK   NUT

....
....
....
....
....

THE MOOVELLOUS MILKY WAY!

HOW TO DRAW AN ASTRONAUT

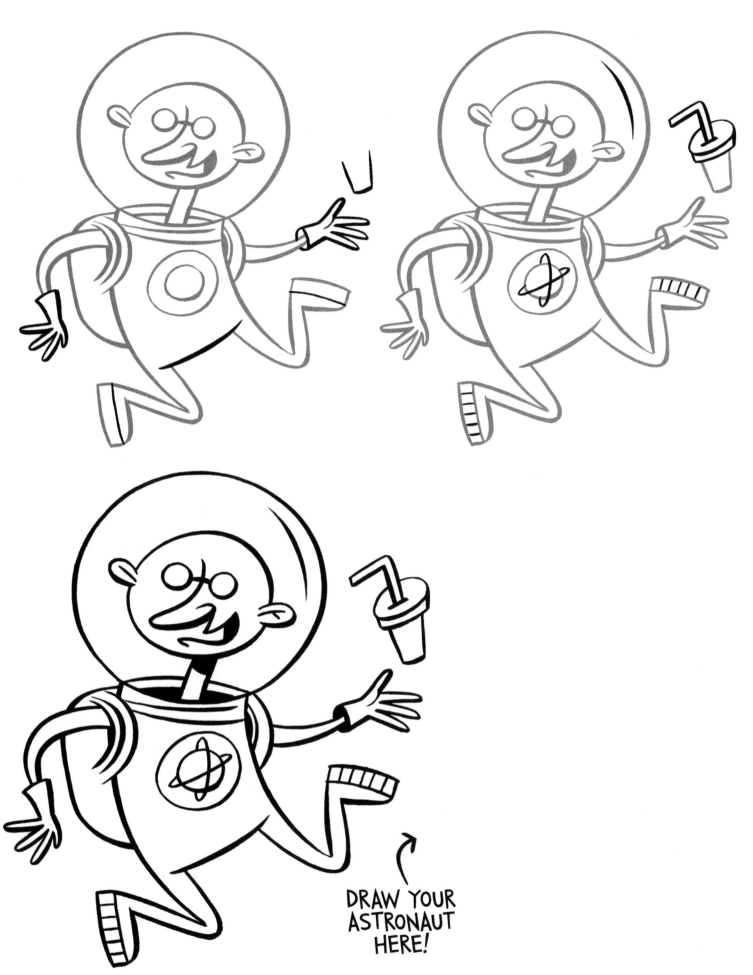

DRAW YOUR
ASTRONAUT
HERE!

245

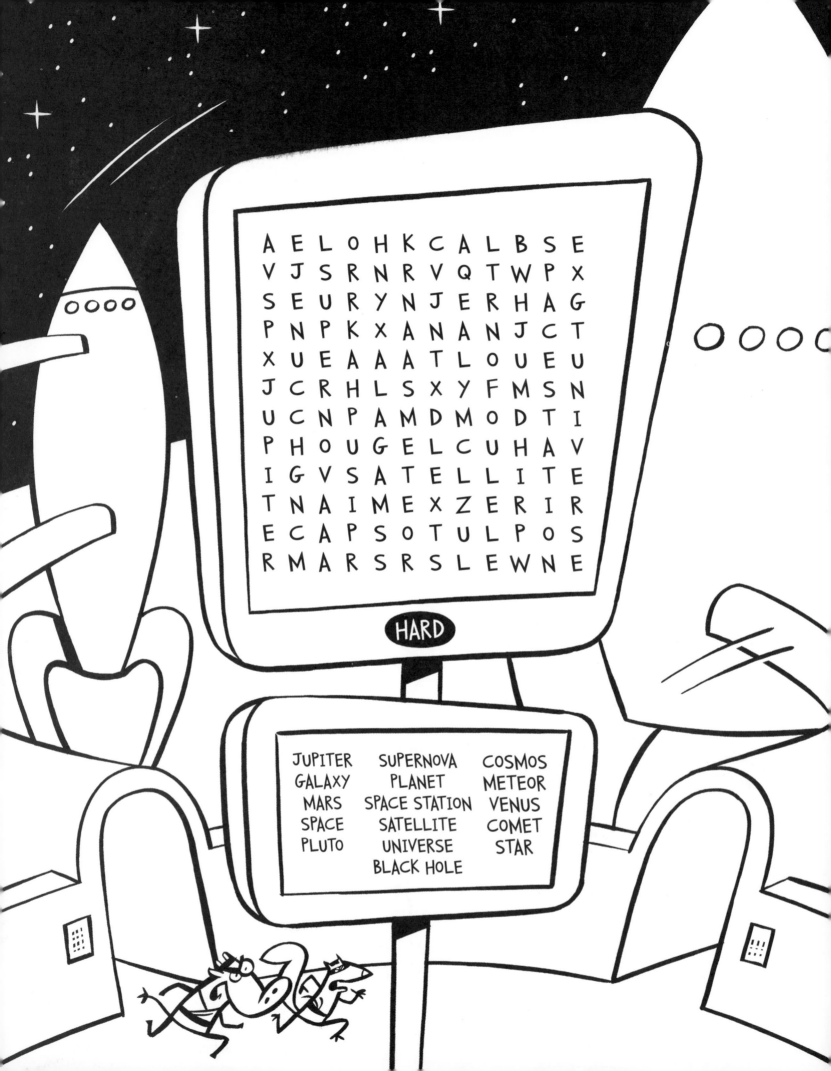

DRAW
THE ROCKET
ON THE
LAUNCHPAD

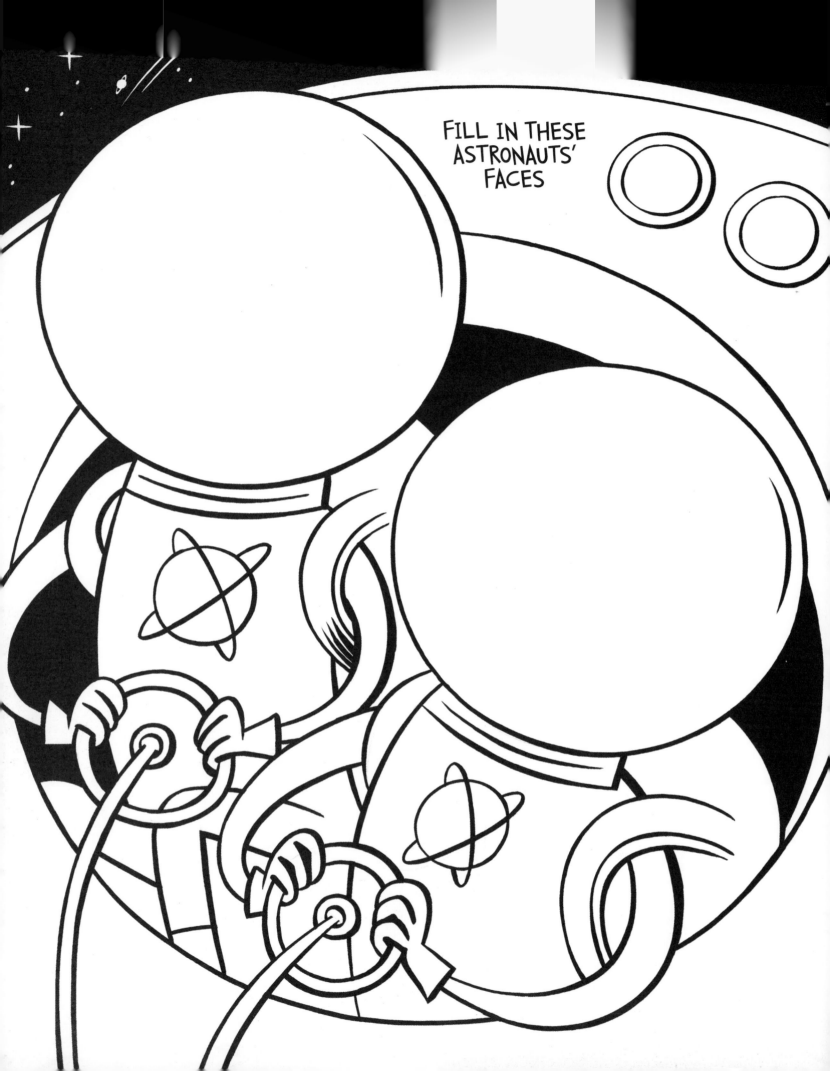

FAIR

FILL IN THE SQUARES SO
EVERY ROW, COLUMN, AND 3×2
BOX CONTAINS THE NUMBERS
1-6.

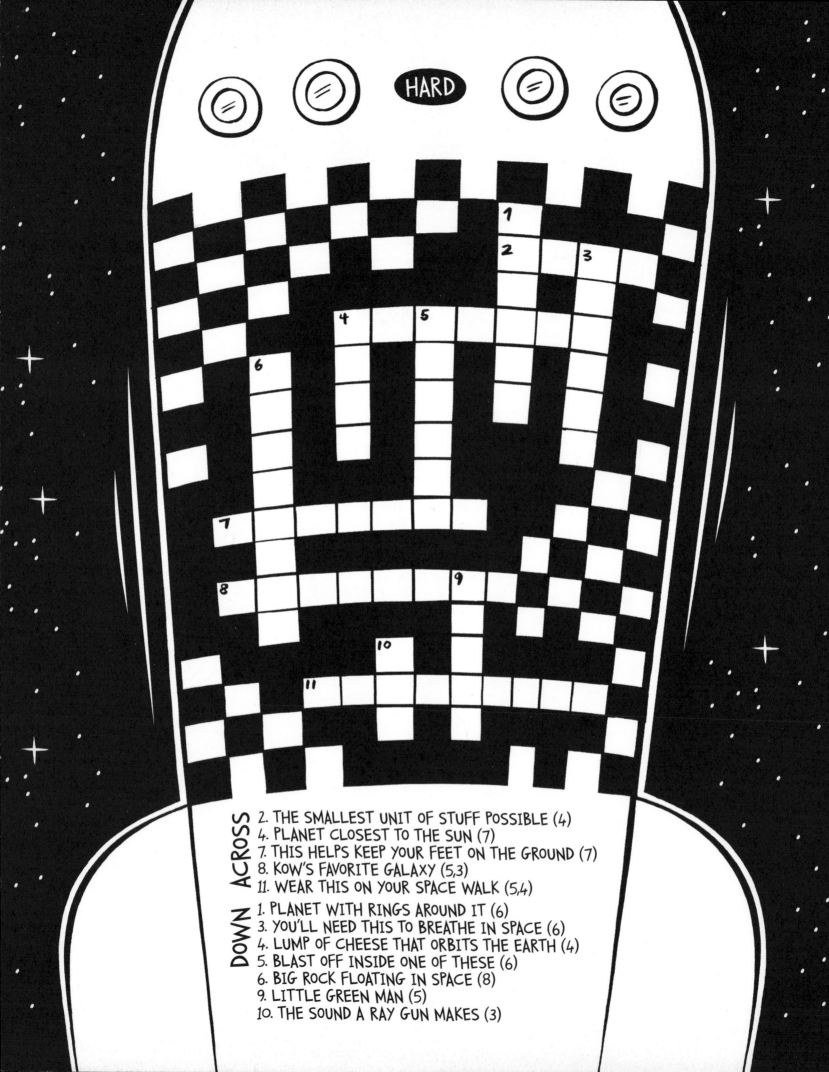

HARD

ACROSS

2. THE SMALLEST UNIT OF STUFF POSSIBLE (4)
4. PLANET CLOSEST TO THE SUN (7)
7. THIS HELPS KEEP YOUR FEET ON THE GROUND (7)
8. KOW'S FAVORITE GALAXY (5,3)
11. WEAR THIS ON YOUR SPACE WALK (5,4)

DOWN

1. PLANET WITH RINGS AROUND IT (6)
3. YOU'LL NEED THIS TO BREATHE IN SPACE (6)
4. LUMP OF CHEESE THAT ORBITS THE EARTH (4)
5. BLAST OFF INSIDE ONE OF THESE (6)
6. BIG ROCK FLOATING IN SPACE (8)
9. LITTLE GREEN MAN (5)
10. THE SOUND A RAY GUN MAKES (3)

WHAT DOES THE MAN IN THE MOON
LOOK LIKE?

WHAT PICTURES CAN YOU MAKE OUT
OF THESE ASTEROIDS?

CONNECT THE STARS TO REVEAL
A NEW CONSTELLATION

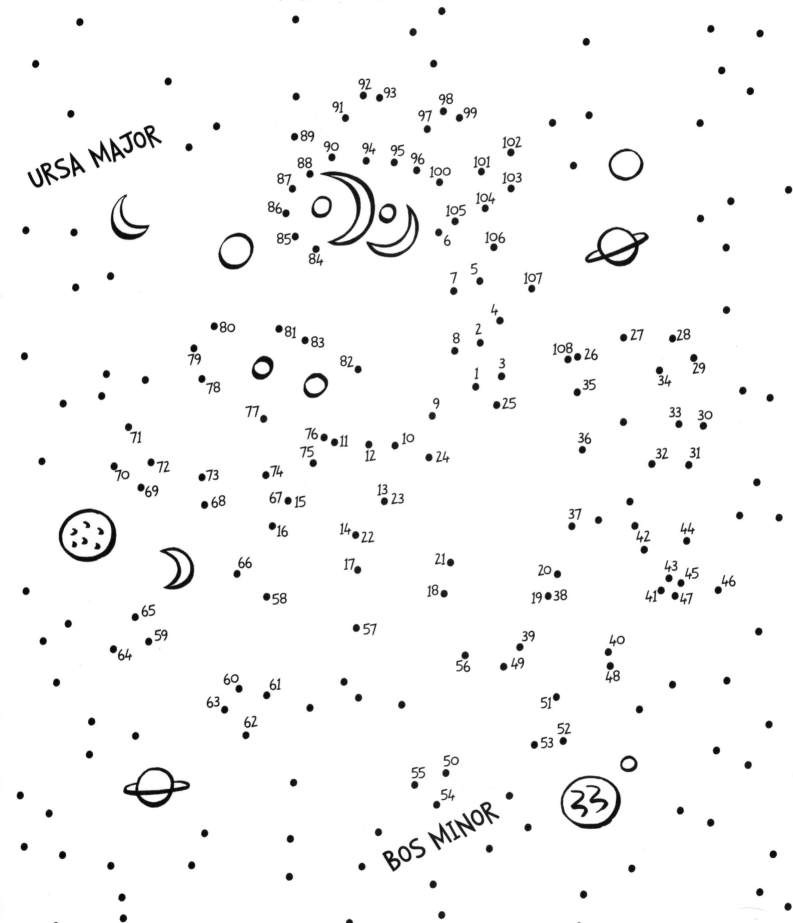

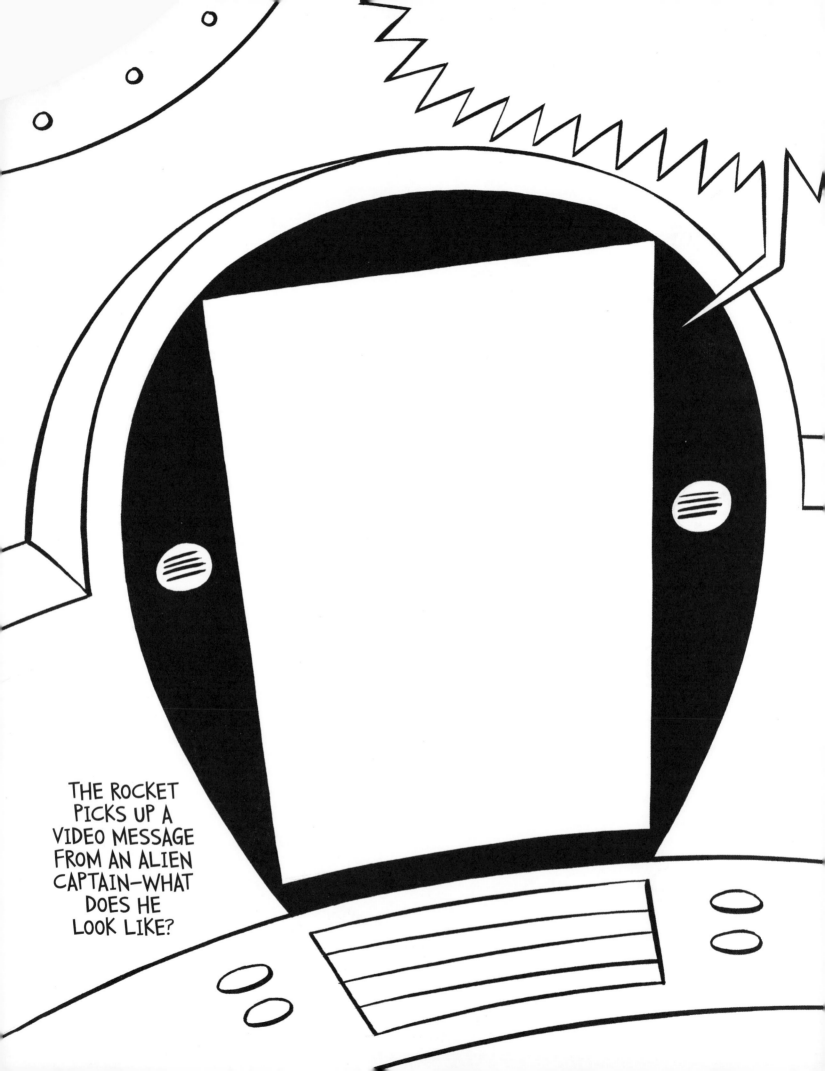

THE ROCKET
PICKS UP A
VIDEO MESSAGE
FROM AN ALIEN
CAPTAIN—WHAT
DOES HE
LOOK LIKE?

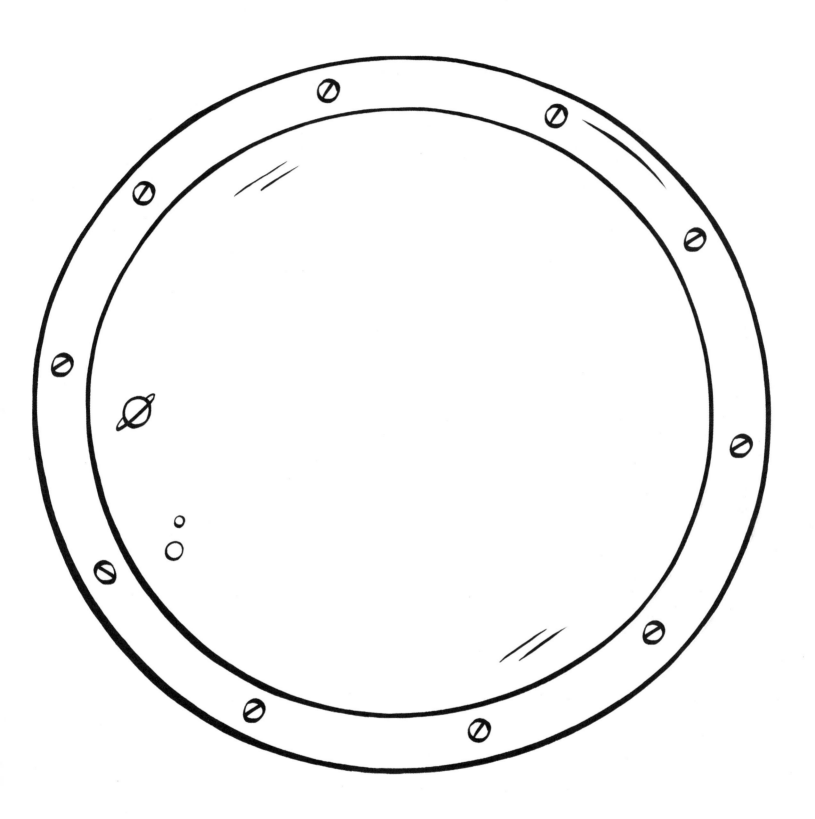

WHAT DOES HIS SPACESHIP LOOK LIKE
THROUGH THE PORTHOLE?

HOW TO DRAW
AN ALIEN

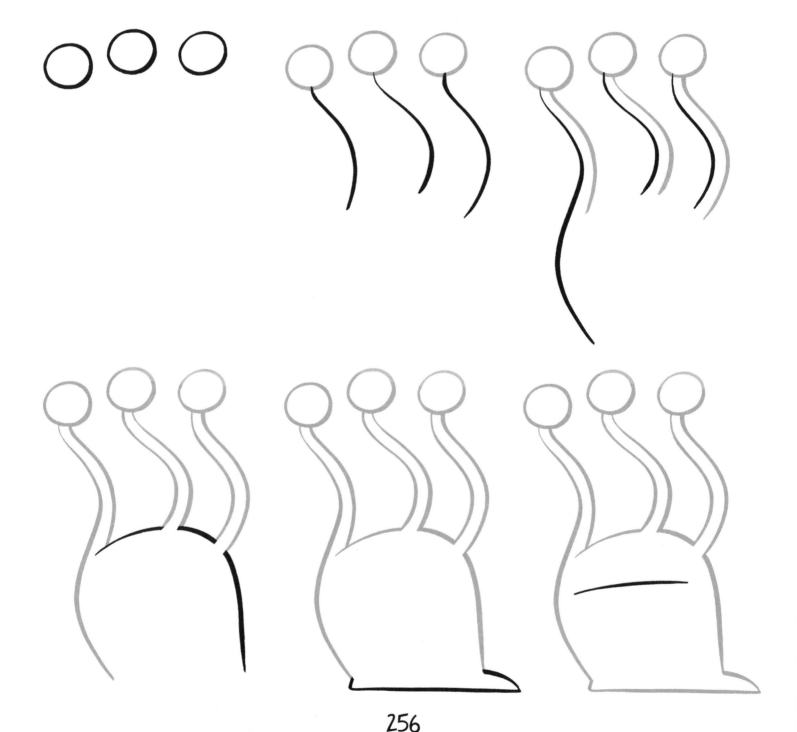

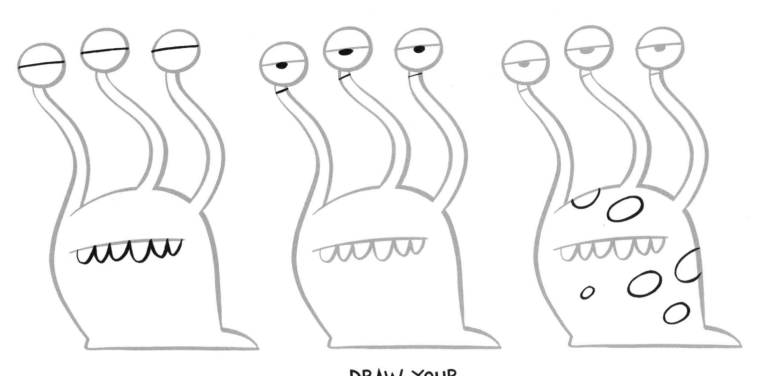

DRAW YOUR
ALIEN HERE!

HOW TO BUILD A UFO!

IT'S A WELL-KNOWN FACT THAT MOST ALIENS USE COMMON KITCHEN APPLIANCES TO BUILD THEIR SPACECRAFT.

FLYING SAUCER

COSMIC COLANDER

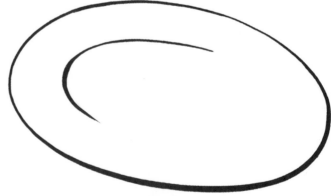

INTER-PLANETARY PLATE

DRAW SOMETHING FROM YOUR KITCHEN AND TURN IT INTO A U.F.O.!

TEST YOUR OBSERVATION SKILLS

1) HOW MANY EYES DID THE WAITER HAVE? ....

2) HOW MANY OF HIS DRINKS HAD UMBRELLAS IN THEM? ....

3) WHAT WAS ON THE SMALL TABLE? ....

4) HOW MANY BOW TIES WERE THERE IN THE PICTURE? ....

5) HOW MANY HUMANS COULD YOU SEE? ....

6) WHAT WAS INSIDE ONE OF THE MOON CRATERS? ....

7) WHAT COLOR WERE PROFESSOR PERIWIG'S SHOES? ....

8) HOW MANY LIGHTS WERE HANGING FROM THE CEILING? ....

9) HOW MANY ASTRONAUTS DID YOU SPOT? ....

10) HOW MANY PLANETS COULD YOU SEE? ....

TOP SECRET

FACT FILE:

"BRIAN"

aka

The Angry Alien

PROFILE:

4 stomachs, 3 eyes, 1 brain cell.

Born in a methane swamp on planet Plink Plonk. Now lives in London.

Loves playing traditonal games like "Paper, Scissors, Ray Gun."

Pet hate : Pets
Favorite food : Earthling soup with crispy toenail croutons and brain juice
Favorite color : Goo
Hobby : Oozing

DRAW THE WEIRDEST ALIEN YOU CAN IMAGINE

WHAT IS THIS U.F.O. BEAMING UP?

HOW TO DRAW A U.F.O.

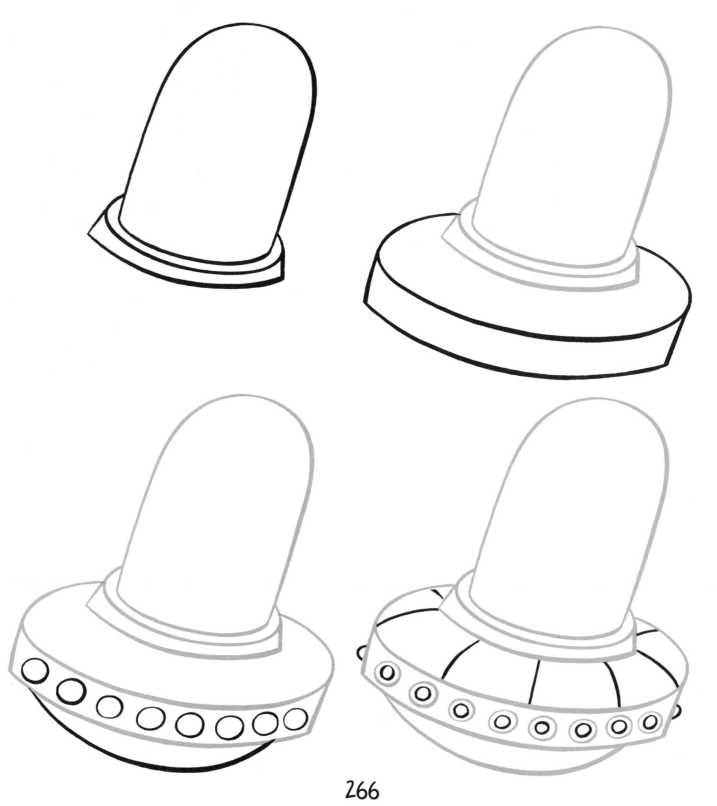

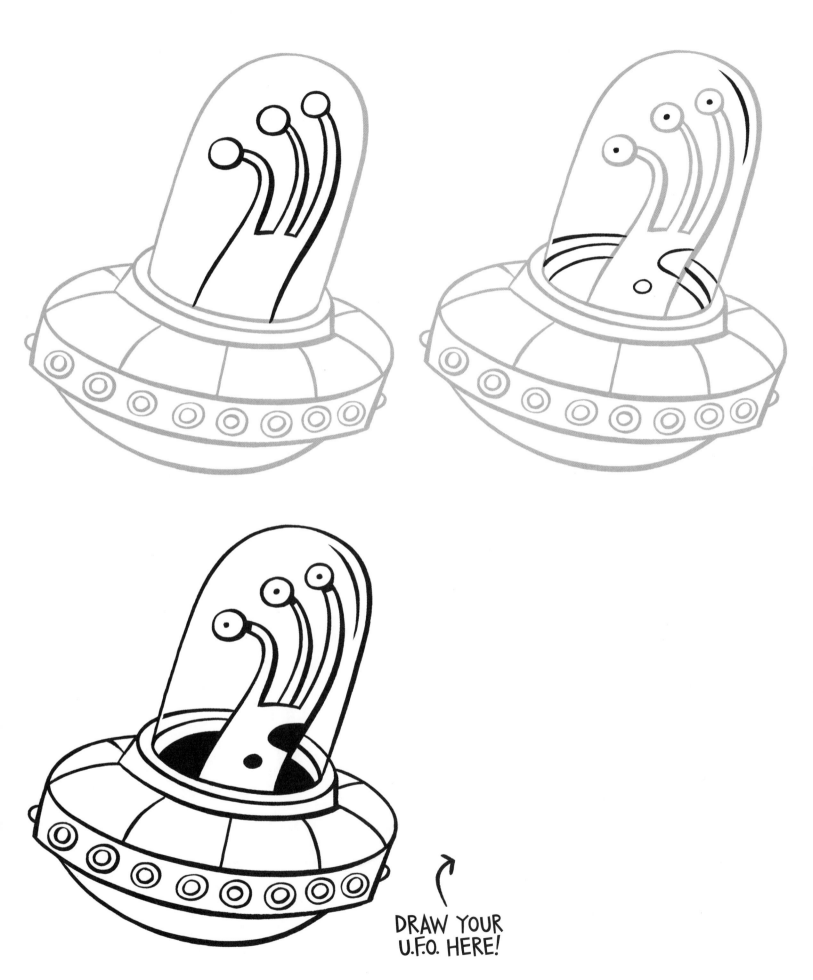

DRAW YOUR
U.F.O. HERE!

SIFT THE SPACE JUNK AND FIND THAT NUT!

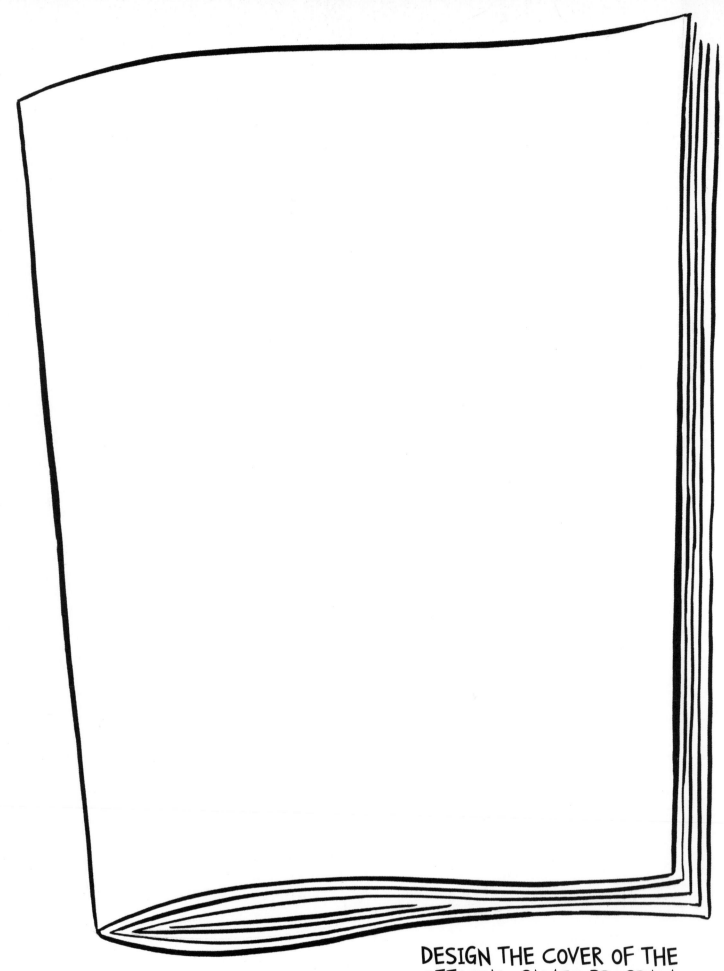

DESIGN THE COVER OF THE
OFFICIAL GAMES PROGRAM

272

WHAT ARE THEY SHOWING
ON THE REPLAY SCREEN?

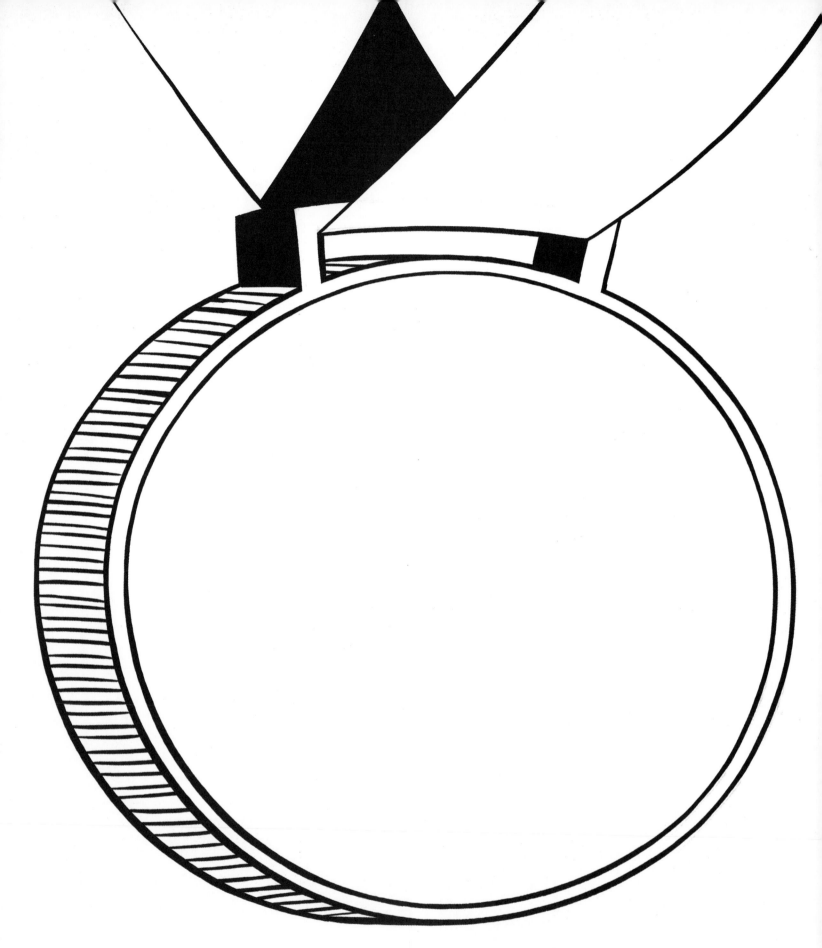

DESIGN A SPECIAL MEDAL
FOR THE ATHLETES

WHAT DOES THE WINNER
OF THE FIRST RACE LOOK LIKE?

DRAW THE FLAG
OF THE WINNER'S
HOME PLANET

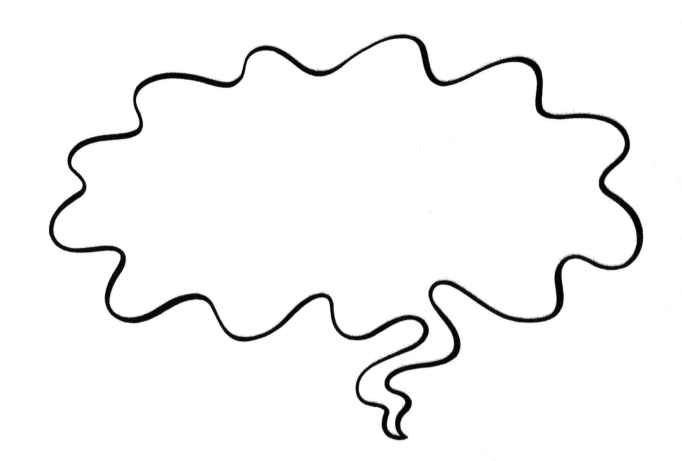

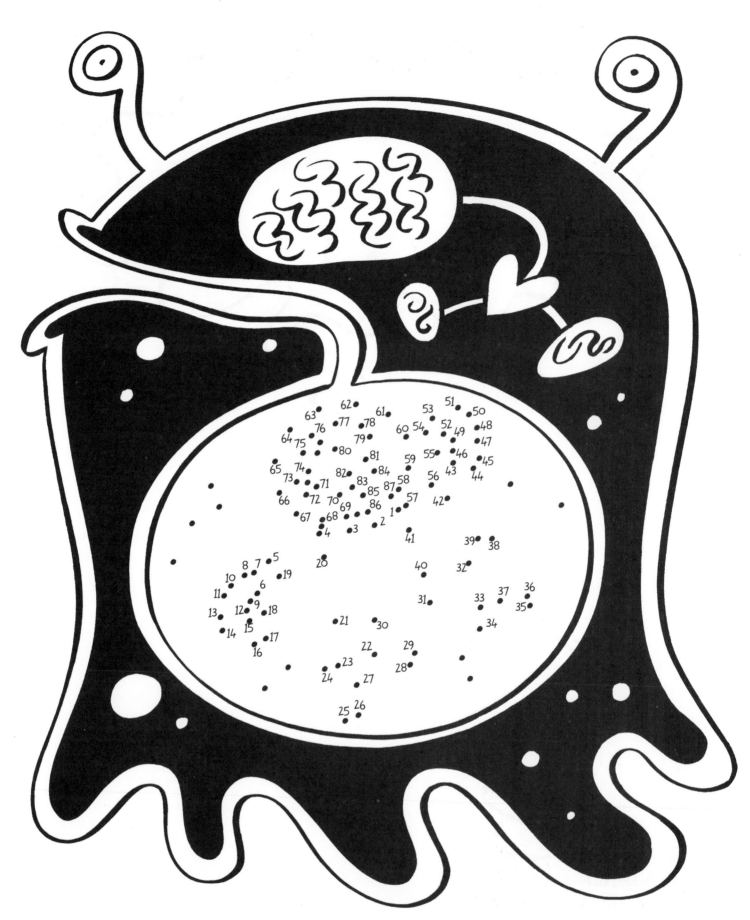

WHAT DID THIS ALIEN ATHLETE
HAVE FOR BREAKFAST?

THIS RUNNER IS WEARING THE FASTEST SHOES
EVER INVENTED—WHAT DO THEY
LOOK LIKE?

FILL IN THE SQUARES SO EVERY ROW, COLUMN, AND BOX CONTAINS THE NUMBERS 1-6.

JUDGE 1 SCORES:
THE NUMBER OF EGGS IN A DOZEN MINUS
THE NUMBER
OF LEGS ON A CHICKEN

JUDGE 2 SCORES:
1) THE NUMBER OF WEEKS IN A YEAR MINUS
THE NUMBER OF DAYS IN A WEEK
2) THE NUMBER OF YEARS IN A DECADE

------- + -------

JUDGE 3 SCORES:
THE NUMBER OF EYES OF JUDGES ONE AND
TWO MINUS THE NUMBER OF MOUTHS OF
JUDGES TWO AND THREE

ANSWER THE QUESTIONS TO   FILL IN THE JUDGES' SCORES

DRAW THE WINNER OF THE
UNIVERSE'S STRONGEST BEING
COMPETITION

DESIGN THE ULTIMATE TROPHY

283

HOW TO MAKE YOUR COMICS TRULY OUT OF THIS WORLD!

IT'S TIME TO ADD
THE ICING
ON THE CAKE

PERSPECTIVE!

THIS SCENE IS OK, BUT WHAT HAPPENS IF WE MIX
THINGS UP A BIT AND START DRAWING FROM A FEW
DIFFERENT ANGLES?

EXTREME CLOSE-UP!

FAR AWAY!

A MIXTURE OF THE TWO!

FROM ABOVE!

FROM BELOW!

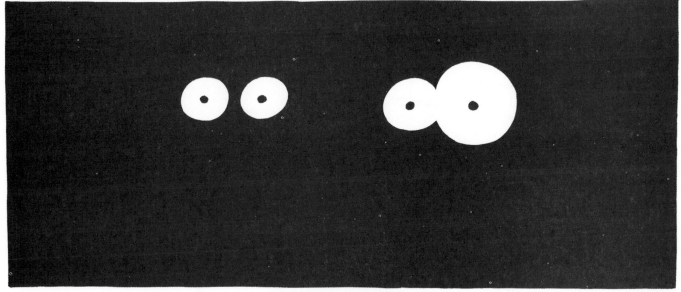

IN THE DARK!

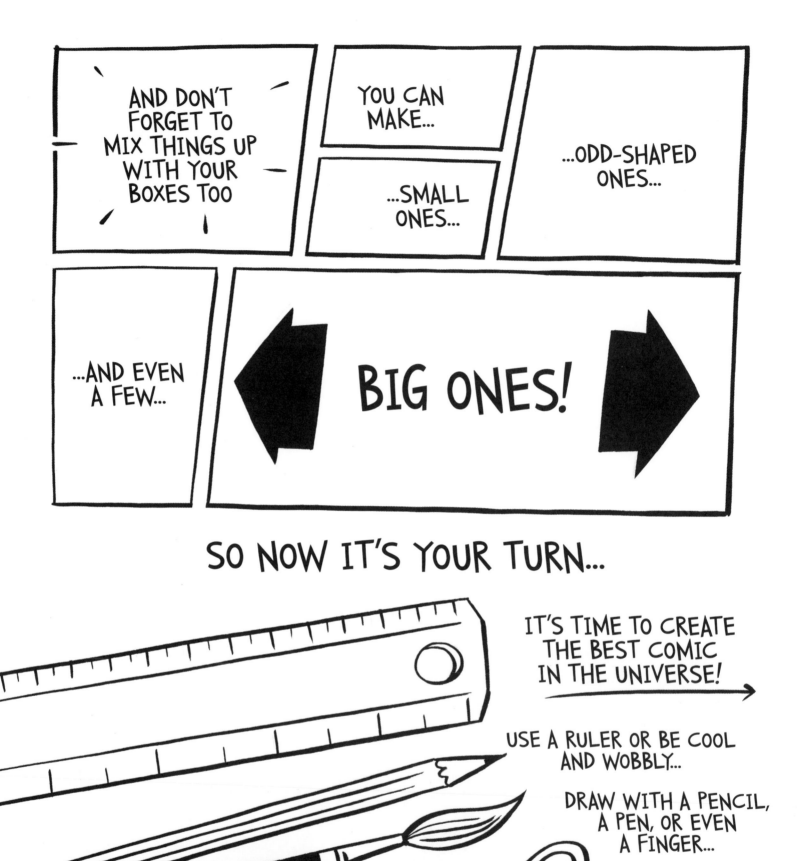

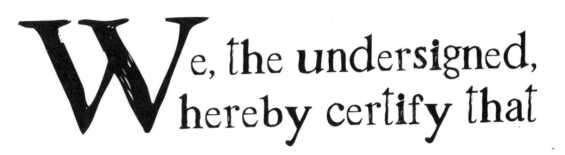

We, the undersigned, hereby certify that

....

has on this day

....

passed the
Kow Kapow
Cartoon Course

Kow Kapow   *BK*

YOUR OFFICIAL
CERTIFICATE!

I CAN'T BELIEVE I DIDN'T THINK OF IT EARLIER

IF MY NUT IS FIRST PRIZE IN THE ULTIMATE ATHLETE COMPETITION...

THEN ALL WE HAVE TO DO IS SIMPLY ENTER THE GAMES...

AND WIN IT BACK!

THERE ARE THOUSANDS OF EVENTS IN HERE— WE MUST BE ABLE TO FIND SOMETHING YOU'RE GOOD AT...

HOW ABOUT TIDDLYWINKS?

I PREFER 40 WINKS

A-HA! GOT IT!

SORRY LADY, BELLY-DANCING RACE OVER

NOW EEZ ONLY ONE EVENT LEFT...

SPOT THE 10 DIFFERENCES!

YOU JOIN US FOR INCREDIBLE SCENES IN THE INTERGALACTIC DECATHLON

CURRENT CHAMPION ZOK THE DESTROYER IS DEDUCTED 10,000 POINTS FOR A SHOELACE VIOLATION

REPLAY

SO AFTER 10 EVENTS THE SCORES ARE NOW TIED AT 19 POINTS!

WE NOW PROCEED TO THE SUDDEN-DEATH ELIMINATOR

THE ULTIMATE TEST OF ATHLETIC SKILL...

RULES

A STARING CONTEST

LET THE BLINK-OFF BEGIN!

ANSWERS!

26 FUNNY FARM SUDOKU

4	5	7	9	6	1	8	2	3
9	1	2	3	4	8	5	7	6
6	8	3	5	2	7	1	4	9
5	3	6	4	1	2	7	9	8
1	9	8	7	3	6	2	5	4
2	7	4	8	5	9	3	6	1
3	4	1	6	7	5	9	8	2
7	6	9	2	8	3	4	1	5
8	2	5	1	9	4	6	3	7

27 FUNNY FARM WORDSEARCH

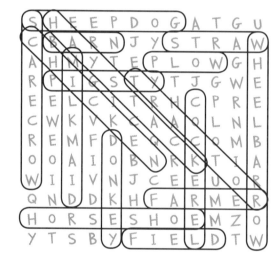

30 CACTUS CROSSWORD

ACROSS
4. NITWITS
5. COWPAT
7. PANTS

DOWN
1. MONKEY NUT SURPRISE
2. GRASS
3. HIC
6. EGGS

32 SPOT THE DIFFERENCE

40 ROBOT WORDSEARCH

46 ROBOT SUDOKU

4	1	2	3
2	3	4	1
1	4	3	2
3	2	1	4

47 EYE TEST WORDSEARCH

67 ZANY ZOO WORDSEARCH

68 ZOO MAP

GNU GARDEN, IGUANA ISLAND, PARROT PERCH, COCKATOO CAFÉ, REPTILE RUMPUS ROOM, PENGUIN PARADISE

77 SPOT THE DIFFERENCE

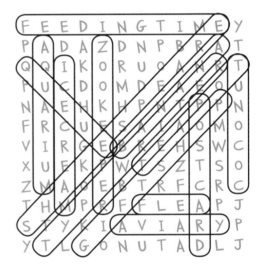

88 SNAKEY CROSSWORD

ACROSS
3. PYTHON
4. ADDER
6. FANGS
7. VENOM

DOWN
1. RATTLESNAKE
2. COBRA
5. HISS

89 POOL SUDOKU

8	2	3	4	1	5	7	9	6
6	5	9	3	7	2	8	4	1
1	7	4	8	9	6	5	2	3
7	1	6	2	5	3	4	8	9
4	8	5	9	6	1	3	7	2
9	3	2	7	4	8	6	1	5
2	6	8	1	3	7	9	5	4
5	9	7	6	2	4	1	3	8
3	4	1	5	8	9	2	6	7

92 MONKEY WORDSEARCH

102 PIRATE SHIP WORDSEARCH

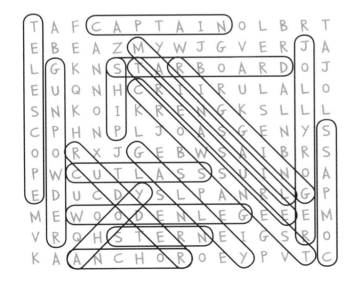

115 PIRATE SPOT THE DIFFERENCE

301

130 FISHY WORDSEARCH

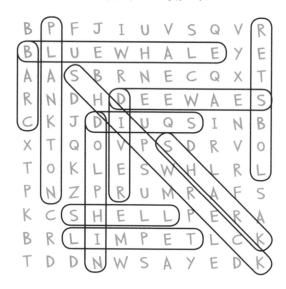

131 FISHY CROSSWORD

ACROSS
1. PROPELLER
4. LIGHTHOUSE
6. SUBMARINE
9. JELLYFISH
10. WATER SKI

DOWN
2. OCTOPUS
3. BLUBBER
5. SNORKEL
7. MERMAID
8. PEARL

158 SPOT THE DIFFERENCE

160 CREEPY CROSSWORD

ACROSS
2. BROOMSTICK
7. DRACULA
8. ELF
9. WALLS
11. WEB
12. CHAINS
13. DUNGEON

DOWN
1. PORTCULLIS
3. MOAT
4. TOWER
5. COFFIN
6. DRAWBRIDGE
10. STAKE

174 DUNGEON DOOR SUDOKU

2	3	4	1
4	1	2	3
1	2	3	4
3	4	1	2

178 SPOT THE DIFFERENCE

182 MONSTER WORDSEARCH

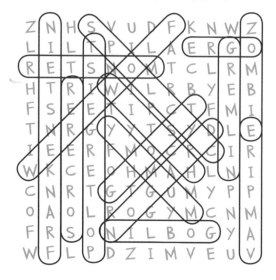

188 SUPER CROSSWORD

ACROSS
3. DEAD END
6. BANK
7. CINEMA
8. ESCALATOR
9. AIRPORT

DOWN
1. SUPERMARKET
2. LIBRARY
4. SKYSCRAPER
5. SEWER

189 SUPER WORDSEARCH

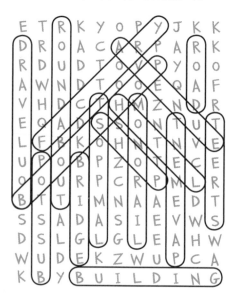

192 SUPERHERO SECRET IDENTITIES

DR. X-RAY ⟶ XAVIER STRONG

RADIOACTIVE RABBIT ⟶ REGGIE BONK

MYSTERY GIRL ⟶ ELOISE GUPPY

BURGER BOY ⟶ HAROLD HARPER

CAPTAIN DISASTER ⟶ CHARLIE PORK

GINGER NINJA ⟶ PETER PERK

202 MUSEUM SPOT THE DIFFERENCE

204 MUSEUM CROSSWORD

ACROSS
6. AUCTION
7. FOSSIL
8. GALLERY

DOWN
1. PAINTING
2. PICASSO
3. VAN GOGH
4. MONA LISA
5. SCULPTURE

205 SAFE CODE

2, 4, 8, 16, 32

1, 8, 15, 22, 29

3, 5, 9, 17, 33

4, 6, 9, 13, 18

208 MENU SUDOKU

4	3	2	1
1	2	4	3
2	1	3	4
3	4	1	2

219 CARS SPOT THE DIFFERENCE

226 SAT NAV WORDSEARCH

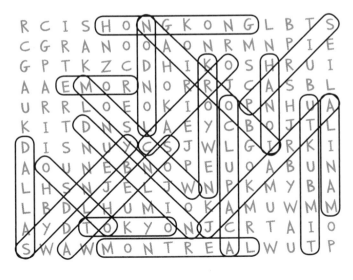

227 CAR RADIO CODE

2, 5, 8, 11, 14

1, 4, 10, 22, 46

1, 3, 4, 7, 11, 18

1, 3, 7, 15, 31

230 ROAD SIGN WORDSEARCH

231 CHECKERED FLAG CROSSWORD

ACROSS	DOWN
3. MECHANIC	1. SPEEDOMETER
5. OVERTAKE	2. HAIRPIN
9. PIT	4. GEARS
10. DRIVER	7. BRAKES
11. PETROL	8. HELMET
13. ENGINE	12. LAP

239 CRAZY QUIZ!

1. A) DEADLY DONUT
2. A) BARMI
3. B) UNIVERSITY OF PERIL
4. B) TREE
5. A) ONE FOR ALL AND ALL FOR PIZZA
6. A) SUDOKU
7. B) UNIDENTIFIED FLYING OBJECT
8. B) RABBITFISH
9.
PARIS, FRANCE
ROME, ITALY
NEW DELHI, INDIA
WASHINGTON, D.C., UNITED STATES
BEIJING, CHINA
TOKYO, JAPAN
NAIROBI, KENYA
OSLO, NORWAY
10. C) JIMMY PEPPER
11. B) HIP HOP
12. SHARKS: BASKING, HAMMERHEAD, TIGER, ZEBRA
NUTS: BRAZIL, MACADAMIA, MONKEY, PINE

246 MILKY WAY WORDSEARCH

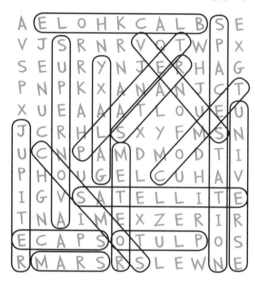

249 SPACESHIP SUDOKU

4	2	1	5	6	3
5	6	3	2	4	1
3	4	5	6	1	2
2	1	6	3	5	4
6	3	4	1	2	5
1	5	2	4	3	6

250 ROCKET CROSSWORD

ACROSS	DOWN
2. ATOM	1. SATURN
4. MERCURY	3. OXYGEN
7. GRAVITY	4. MOON
8. MILKY WAY	5. ROCKET
11. SPACE SUIT	6. ASTEROID
	9. ALIEN
	10. ZAP

262 OBSERVATION TEST

1) THREE EYES
2) TWO DRINKS
3) A BOWL OF NUTS
4) THREE BOW TIES
5) FOUR, INCLUDING PROFESSOR PERIWIG
6) AN ALIEN
7) BLACK
8) TWO LIGHTS
9) THREE (HUMAN) ASTRONAUTS
10) SIX, INCLUDING THE PLANET THE CAFÉ IS ON

280 ALIEN SUDOKU

2	5	6	4	1	3
1	3	4	2	5	6
3	1	2	5	6	4
6	4	5	1	3	2
4	6	1	3	2	5
5	2	3	6	4	1

281 JUDGES' SCORES
SCORES : 10, 45, 10, 4

296 SPOT THE DIFFERENCE